I0798675

Dr. Annie Dove Denmark

Dr. Annie Dove Denmark

South Carolina's First Female College President

Kathryn Copeland

edited by Anne Marie Martin & Linda Millwood, with Bethany Wade

Foreword by Reverend E. Leon Smith

The History Press

Published by The History Press
Charleston, SC 29403
www.historypress.net

First published 2011

Manufactured in the United States

ISBN 978.1.60949.212.0

Library of Congress Cataloging-in-Publication Data
Copeland, Kathryn.
Dr. Annie Dove Denmark, South Carolina's first female college president / Kathryn Copeland ; edited by Anne Marie Martin and Linda Millwood.
p. cm.
Includes index.
ISBN 978-1-60949-212-0
1. Denmark, Annie Dove. 2. Anderson College (Anderson, S.C.)--Presidents--Biography. 3. Women community college presidents--South Carolina--Biography. I. Martin, Anne Marie. II. Millwood, Linda. III. Title.
LD6501.A6C67 2011
378.757'25--dc22
[B]
2010050115

Notice: The information in this book is true and complete to the best of our knowledge. It is offered without guarantee on the part of the author or The History Press. The author and The History Press disclaim all liability in connection with the use of this book.

This project has been very much a labor of love for those involved.
Kathryn Copeland spent many years working on her manuscripts, but she did not live to see the project come to fruition.
Our involvement in the project is due to the work and vision of Dr. Joyce Wood, our colleague, teacher, friend and mentor. Without her drive, the manuscript would continue to sit on our archive shelves, a treasure accessible to us but available to few others.
This publication is dedicated to them with gratitude and appreciation for the gift they have given us.

Contents

Contents

Foreword

The study of history teaches us the hopeful reality of how capable and charismatic leaders emerge at pivotal moments to inspire and change the course of events. Dr. Annie Dove Denmark was just such a person for a small liberal arts college in South Carolina. Caught in the vortex of the economic Depression of the 1930s, an oppressive debt and declining student enrollment, Anderson College, Anderson, South Carolina, was on the precipice of closing its doors. Into this challenging stream of time stepped a remarkable woman who, in the words of Esther 4:14, "came to the kingdom for such a time as this."

When I walked across the stage in 1959 to receive my junior college diploma and hear my induction into the Denmark Society,[1] there was never the thought that one day I would get to meet Dr. Denmark, much less that I would serve the First Baptist Church of Goldsboro, North Carolina, of which she was a member. Dr. Denmark had returned to Goldsboro, her home, to be near her family. My wife, Martha, and I were truly blessed by the many years we experienced her glowing personality and seasoned wisdom. We grew to understand why relatives as well as friends came to call her lovingly "Aunt Dovie."

Leadership comes to those who prepare. Dr. Denmark was well prepared for the challenges she would face. The discipline she learned in the study of music, the sacrifice she endured from poor salaries in other college settings and the enlightened Christian values that her dynamic faith instilled in her served to shape an outstanding person of stature and leadership.

In some ways it is fair to say that Dr. Denmark was elected president of the college in 1927 after the trustees had searched "in vain for a man who would be suitable," as the *Anderson Daily Mail* stated in 1941. Her remarkable leadership for the next twenty-five years gives testimony to the marvelous leadership skills of women in all facets of life. Becoming the first female president of a college in South Carolina, Dr. Denmark took the reins of a college on the way to closing its doors. Today, Anderson University is a thriving liberal arts college with a bright future—a future that would not exist without the indomitable and tenacious spirit of Dr. Denmark.

As her pastor for many years, I was always impressed with her wonderful spirit of openness and progressive thinking. Spending several weeks of each summer at Chautauqua Lake in New York provided the opportunity to meet and hear some of the sentinel minds of her generation. She proudly announced to me one day that she had all the books that Dr. Harry Emerson Fosdick had published. Later, she gave me many of Dr. Fosdick's books, which I treasure today. Her collection of pictures of Madonnas was often passed on to others in the many notebooks she prepared for her family and friends. Even in her senior years, she would be found at her desk compiling encouraging messages with appropriate art for those whom she loved and respected. Her remarkable mind would not rest on the laurels of yesterday's memories. She was truly alive all the days that she lived.

As I look back on the years of serving as Dr. Denmark's pastor, it becomes very clear that this opportunity was a grace gift from God. How improbable that a graduate of the institution that she literally saved from extinction would serve as her pastor for many years and stand in the pulpit at her memorial service to bear witness to her life. I can still hear her reminding me of some words of Ralph Waldo Emerson: "Sow a thought and you reap an action; sow an act and you reap a habit; sow a habit and you reap a character; sow a character and you reap a destiny." I would suspect that the students at Anderson College heard these words in chapel many times. Her story must be told and retold to inspire coming generations that all things are possible for those who have the audacity to dream the impossible dream!

Reverend E. Leon Smith

Acknowledgements

Our heartfelt thanks and appreciation go to the following individuals:

Dr. Margaret Wooten for her invaluable advice and for her assistance in editing this wonderful story.

The Denmark family for their time, remembrances, permission to use family pictures and their kindness to us as we reveal a portion of the life of their beloved Aunt Dovie.

Charlotte Hendley Badger and Helen Hendley Donnell,[2] for the pictures and memorabilia they kindly donated to the archives and for this endeavor, for telling us wonderful stories of the friends they remember so well and for Appendices D and E, which they wrote in tribute to those friends.

The Reverend E. Leon Smith, graduate of Anderson College, where he was honored with induction into the Denmark Society and Dr. Denmark's pastor in her final years, for his graciousness in providing our foreword.

Kent Millwood, library director, for proofreading, for his encouragement of our project and for his forbearance as we infringed on our regular duties at home and at work.

The entire library staff of the Thrift Library for their assistance with research and for taking up the slack when time was short.

The Anderson University administration for the funding that made this project possible.

Dr. Joyce Wood for beginning this project and for allowing us to help finish it and bring Dean Copeland's story about the remarkable Dr. Denmark to publication.

Introduction

On February 14, 2011, Anderson University will celebrate its centennial. Founded by citizens of Anderson and supported by the Southern Baptist Convention, Anderson College was begun as a senior college for girls. A preparatory school for girls was added, and it was reorganized as the first junior college in South Carolina in 1929, admitting boys as day students in 1930, returning to senior college status in 1990 and gaining university status in 2006.

During its first one hundred years, Anderson University has had twelve presidents. The fifth of those presidents, Dr. Annie Dove Denmark, has the distinction of having served for a quarter of a century and of being the first female president not only of Anderson College but in the state of South Carolina as well. Arriving at Anderson College in 1917 as a music teacher, Dr. Denmark was appointed dean of women in 1925 and president in 1928, taking on the task of leading an institution with a large debt through a difficult financial period. The college not only survived but also prospered under her guidance. When Dr. Denmark retired in 1953, Anderson College was free of debt, and she had been able to build up, through good and careful management, a savings account for her beloved college.

The college and its faculty, staff, students and alumni returned Dr. Denmark's affection. In those days, Anderson College was a home away from home for many of the students. Faculty and staff, including Dr. Denmark, lived on campus in the dormitories with the students, eating at the table with them in the dining hall, going on outings and attending church with them. Miss Annie Dove dedicated all her energies, intelligence and talents to the skillful administration of Anderson College, ensuring that thousands of students—all "her children"—had the opportunity to obtain an education that concentrated on the spirit as well as the mind.

Often, opportunities present themselves in unlikely places, as seems to be the case for both the presidency of Dr. Denmark and the publication of this manuscript. While you will learn more about Dr. Denmark and her many accomplishments throughout this collection of documents, a note on the main manuscript by Kathryn Copeland is certainly in order.

The main manuscript for this book, "When Green Grew the Ivy," is part of a collection of manuscripts for a biography on Miss Denmark as told by her friend and colleague, Dean Kathryn Copeland. This story gives the reader a view of the life of an extraordinary woman who prospered in a time when women were considered by many to be capable only of running a household. Undertaken after Dr. Denmark's retirement, Dean Copeland went through numerous drafts and revisions of the biography, but it was never published. Eventually, the manuscript drafts came to the Anderson University archives, where they have been housed for many years.

The copy of the manuscript we selected for the main body of the book was one Dr. Denmark herself actually read and edited in 1968. You will note that any comments in the body of the manuscript that are bracketed are Dr. Denmark's own thoughts and corrections. The letter she sent back to Dean Copeland with the edited manuscript has been reproduced in Appendix A; in it, you can see Dr. Denmark's characteristic modesty. The final chapter, "...And Then She Taught," is from a later manuscript, written after Dr. Denmark's death. The manuscript has been left in its original form, and all grammar, sentence structure and phrasing is original. The only editorial inclusion, besides Dr. Denmark's comments in brackets, is a series of endnotes, which provides more information and clarification of some persons, places and events. Along with Dr. Denmark's letter, you will find further appendices offering more detailed information on a few specific individuals who were very much a part of Dr. Denmark's life.

While this compilation is not the "end all, be all" of publications on Dr. Denmark's life, we hope that it can provide a starting point for future work and research. Dr. Denmark may have been by nature modest, but she was truly a very accomplished woman, far ahead of her time, who deserves to be remembered and honored.

When Green Grew the Ivy

Chapter I

"Ivy Walls Do Not a Prison Make"

A woman that feareth the Lord, she shall be praised. Give her of the fruit of her hands; and let her own works praise her in the gates.
—Proverbs 31:30–31

It was Valentine's Day, 1953. On the night before, distinguished visitors began checking into the hotels in the city of Anderson, South Carolina. Early that bright winter morning automobiles lined the tree-shaded Boulevard and jammed the driveway circling the administration building of Anderson College. By mid-morning they filled the parking spaces near the red brick buildings with their classic white columns and ivy-covered walls. Crowds thronged the doorways.

In the spacious halls dignitaries in impressive academic regalia formed a line of march. From the organ pealed the victorious strains, "All Glory, laud and honor," as the robed choir led the processional.

At the head of the long line of college and university presidents and other officials marched an erect woman of sixty-five, Annie Dove Denmark. On that Valentine's day, college and community celebrated the twenty-fifth anniversary of Dr. Denmark's presidency of Anderson College and the forty-second birthday of the college.[3]

The presidency had been thrust upon Miss Denmark in [January] 1928. She had not sought this honor, but frankly admitted she accepted it because she loved the college and could not bear to see it die. When three men, to whom the trustees turned, declined the position, the trustees urged Miss Denmark to serve as acting president to succeed R.H. Holliday, a member of the faculty, who served for a period of three months.

This picture of Dr. Denmark is from the 1929 *Sororian*, page 10.

With the forthrightness and frankness of youth, she refused to accept anything less than full authority for what was at that time a small, financially unstable senior college for women. Her letter declining to serve as temporary head warned that the college was in danger of giving out to the public the impression that "We have an experiment station here to try out presidents."

Some readers of South Carolina newspapers apparently were shocked when they read an announcement in January, 1928, of the election of a woman as president of Anderson College.

Indeed, one of these readers, the wife of a prominent South Carolina pastor, unhesitatingly voiced her opposition. "The next thing you know that woman college president will be asking to speak in our churches and at our State Baptist Convention. Our church is conservative. Down South, women don't stand in the pulpit and speak—not in South Carolina."

The trustees admitted that they had taken Miss Denmark from behind her desk as a busy dean of women and placed her in the president's office because no man dared risk his prestige with the insecure position. The Baptists of South Carolina had four church-related colleges for women besides Furman University for men.[4] Denominational support divided among five institutions was negligible, and Anderson College's endowment was infinitesimal. In the face of both feminine and masculine pessimism, Miss Denmark undertook the formidable task.

On that anniversary, twenty-five years later, representatives from civic, church, and educational groups saluted Dr. Denmark as a successful college executive. She had not only spoken, as prophesied, in South Carolina churches from the mountains to the sea, but she had presided as vice president of the State Baptist Convention as the first woman in its history elected to a state office.

During her fourth of a century as a college president she had stood before many other groups: starry-eyed college seniors at commencement

Anderson College students sit on the campus swings, which are a favorite place for reading, talking and studying. This picture is from the 1942 *Columns*, page 7.

convocations, Southern Baptist leaders in annual sessions, and educators gathered to discuss scholarly papers.

During her administration no buildings of brick and mortar were erected; emphasis [distinction made between the transient and the eternal] was placed on the building of character into the lives of girls and boys. She left Anderson College free from debt, occupying a distinctive place in the educational program of the state and assured of increasing financial support [$985,000] from the denomination with which it is connected.

Retiring in June of 1953 she became a legendary figure. She left the college just as a new wave of mass education and machinery was engulfing educational institutions. The college with which her name was associated for so many years is now forced to limit its enrollment although new buildings are mushrooming all over the campus under the leadership of its seventh president, Dr. John Edward Rouse. But with Dr. Denmark's retirement an era had passed.

Perhaps today's dedicated but still underpaid teachers working in overcrowded classrooms are not too different from those who sought to make a home-away-from home on a college campus for young people entrusted to their care when the century was young and there were no "lost week-ends" between September and the Christmas holidays.

The Denmark story gives glimpses of life within and without the ivy walls as it seeks to reveal the influences that led to a career in religious education and the compensations that come with retirement for a woman who spent almost four decades [plus 4 yrs.] working with young people. It was in North Carolina that the Denmark story began over eighty years ago.

CHAPTER 2

What Is Your Name?

A good name is rather to be chosen than great riches.
—Proverbs 22:1

"What is your name?"

For many years President Denmark chose this subject for her opening chapel talk to each new group of Anderson College students. "I have been emphasizing this question of names ever since you arrived," Miss Denmark told the college students. "Jesus asked a person, 'What is thy name?' This is the first question you were asked when you set foot on the campus."

The following quotation is taken from the notebook of a former student, Mrs. James Howard (Ruth Hill, 1928):

"When you graduate from Anderson College your name ought to have some content and meaning. The alumnae directory is full of names of girls who have lived gloriously. You can write across your own forehead a name that will be an honor to yourself and an honor to those who gave you life and to your college with which you have chosen to cast your lot."

Dr. Denmark called the names of some of the Anderson College students who became missionaries: Myra P. Anderson, 1916–20; Sara Lou Bobo Patterson, 1917–21; and Maud McDaniel, 1917–21. [Viola Campbell?]

She used the name of Myra P. Anderson as an example of a student who had brought honor to Anderson College. Myra, a graduate of the senior class of 1920, gave herself to Japan as a missionary after her graduation from Scarritt College. Under a Methodist Board she served a long term, returning to her homeland only a short time before her death from cancer.

Miss Denmark said admiringly of Myra:

"Now I am thinking of a girl who walked into Anderson College in 1916. She gave us a name. It was just a name given her by a family up in the mountains of Oconee County, South Carolina. She began right off to clothe that name with meaning," Miss Denmark said of Myra, who was president of the Student Government Association and student assistant to the administrative offices.

"Her name is distinguished in the roll of Anderson College alumnae, and she made it so. She was thorough and accurate in scholarship. She was clean and straightforward. She never broke a rule. She was faithful in meeting the larger obligations of college life, showing a keen interest in the privileges and responsibilities of her life here. She cared little for dress, almost too little. She was genial and likable and serious in her work. She graduated with as high honors as the college could give her. She gave herself away to other people. And she is loved and honored by every succeeding generation of Anderson College students.

"Myra P. Anderson is just one. There are scores of other outstanding names in our college directory which are clothed with distinction. It is just as easy—easier—to clothe a name with dishonor. Are you content to leave your name as it is today? Unless a person is flexible and knows how to change, she might as well pack her trunk and go home. People who graduate cum laude are always few in number, but every one of you here today can develop character of the highest type. You can make your contribution to the larger life of Anderson College.

"Our names for the most part have no definite content of their own. Your surname you inherited from your father and grandfather. We can't choose our given names. When we are babies we have to take what is given us. We can't talk back. It is left to each of you to pack your names with such meaning as you may choose. Are you content to leave your name as it is today?"

The 1926 graduating class of Anderson College lists the name of Annie Dove Denmark. While teaching piano at the college she completed courses which made it possible for her to receive the A.B. degree at Anderson College.

She never received an earned graduate degree. Furman University conferred the honorary degree of Doctor of Letters upon her in 1941.

Miss Denmark speaks with pride of her name on the Anderson College alumni list. Admirers of the former college president have called her name one of the most distinguished.

It is not difficult to imagine in the ancestry of Annie Dove Denmark the daring Vikings or Danes who lived and warred in the stirring sagas of the North. The neighbors in the new western land must have found the Danish name of her paternal ancestors unpronounceable. It was much simpler to call these Danish settlers the Denmark brothers.

Annie Dove Denmark's father was Willis Arthur Denmark, who had lived in Goldsboro before the days of the Civil War and had watched it grow from a cross roads village to an important city. He was Wayne County tax collector for thirty-three years and served Goldsboro as an alderman.

He was superintendent of the Sunday School and senior deacon of the Second Baptist Church in Goldsboro for more than twenty [30] years. A marker in front of the old Second Baptist church building names W.A. Denmark as one of the leaders in the establishment of the church. The church also dedicated a bell to him.

Willis Arthur Denmark was born September 25, 1850, and died July 18, 1926. He was married twice, first to Clarissa Boyette. She died when their child, Mary Clyde, was two years old. On December 30, 1880, eleven months after the death of his first wife, Willis Arthur married again. His second wife was Sara Emma Boyette, sister of Clarissa.

Sara Emma teased her husband as long as he lived, saying that she would not have married him if it had not been for the baby. She said she knew that some one else would marry him and she was determined to have Mary Clyde.

Sara Emma often told her children how she adored her older sister. It had never occurred to her that Sister would leave her and she was heartbroken. There were only the two Boyette children and Willis Arthur Denmark married each [both] of them.

The first two children of Sara Emma and Willis Arthur Denmark were boys, Edward Cobb and Walter Clark. The Denmarks lost a little girl and then Annie Dove was born on September 29, 1887. Their last child was another boy, Robert Lewis.

Willis Denmark's first wife was called "Sweet Mama." Annie Dove said she grew up believing that every family had a Mama and a Sweet Mama. She recalls that her maternal grandmother lived with them and was called "Mammy."

Dove was a family name. Her maternal grandfather was William E. Boyette. He was killed in the seven days fight around Richmond. He had a sister Emily Boyette who married James Dove.

Annie Dove was bred on stories of the Civil War. Her mother was born in 1853 [1857] and remembered when Sherman came to Goldsboro. He went through their home, pillaging it of valuables and food, while she hid under the bed. Annie Dove's father was too young to take part in the Civil War, but his two older brothers participated and one of them was killed.

The father, Joseph Dixon Denmark, and the mother of Willis Arthur Denmark lived next door to their son and had a big family. Patience was the name of the mother of Willis Arthur. All the children got together on May 28, Joseph Dixon's birthday. Annie Dove remembers the birthday as a time when plums, peaches, and cherries were ripe.

Willis Arthur's sister Fannie had six boys and no daughter. Aunt Fannie Edwards lived in the country. She came into Goldsboro for a visit when Annie Dove was a month old. She returned home and was dead in a week's time from what was then called croup colic but today would probably be diagnosed as acute appendicitis. After Aunt Fannie's death there was some thought of changing the Annie Dove to Fannie.

This picture of the Denmark family is believed to have been taken on the fiftieth wedding anniversary of Emma and Willis Denmark. The family is as follows: (top row) Nancy Denmark, Walter Denmark, Beulah Denmark, Clyde Crawford, Edward Denmark; (middle row) Robert Denmark, Annie Dove Denmark, Emma Boyette Denmark, Willis Denmark, Mary Crawford, John Crawford Sr.; (bottom row) Berta Crawford Hamilton, Ed Denmark, Willis Denmark Jr., Virginia Crawford Henderson, John Crawford Jr. *Courtesy of the Denmark family.*

The name remained Annie Dove, the family calling her by the two names. At school she was Annie. She is Aunt Dovie to many of the alumnae of early years. She acquired this name when her niece, Roberta Crawford, taught science for a short time at Anderson College. Today she is Dovie to her close friends.

She is most frequently addressed by the titles Miss Denmark or Dr. Denmark, but is often called Miss Annie or Miss Annie Dove. Her long-time friends, Dr. A.L. Smethers and Mrs. Smethers, of Anderson, affectionately called her "Dennie." Significantly her long tenure of service at Anderson College resulted in her receiving many letters with the salutation "Dear Dr. Anderson."

CHAPTER 3

"You Don't Have to Stay the Way You Are"

And Jesus increased in wisdom and stature and in favor with God and man.
—Luke 2:52

A preacher asked a six-year old girl, "Daughter, who made you?"

The girl replied, "God made me so big (illustrating with her hands) and I growed the rest."

This is a favorite story of Miss Denmark's. "There is a real philosophy in that child's answer," she has commented. "Someone has said that what we are is God's gift to us. What we make of ourselves is our gift to God."

She relates that once Mark Twain was sent thirteen subjects, topics for an address. From these the ones in charge of the occasion were to make the choice. He wrote [in a postscript], "It makes little difference which topic you select; the address will be the same in any case."

"Growth" is a favorite theme for her [Miss D's] many addresses. She insists that it makes no difference what subject she is assigned for one of her speeches; she always talks on the topic, "Growth."

When The Review and Expositor, a Baptist Theological Quarterly, edited by the faculty of the Southern Baptist Theological Seminary, carried an article written by Miss Denmark, entitled "Life Expanding" it was copied from an address on the subject, "Growth," given as the commencement address by her at the Woman's Missionary Union Training School in Louisville, Kentucky.

"If you grow, you have to outgrow something," she frequently reminded Anderson College students. "I think this applies to some of our inherited ideas of right and wrong behavior."

She said to the young people, "Student government is a growing process. What you will be, you are now becoming."

"You don't have to stay the way you are today. God's caterpillars are being changed to butterflies. God's bulbs are becoming God's daffodils and flowers. God's world is full of romantic possibilities of growth. In each of you are untold possibilities. You are responsible before God for a personality whose flame will never go out."

Always in her talks Miss Denmark emphasized that no one should cease growing. "We are not finished products," she said. "We are Becomers. Our objective is to be like Christ.

"How much do our faith and understanding grow from day to day?" She earnestly posed this question to students. "God made us to grow! Our hearts grieve when we see a young body stunted and dwarfed by accident or misfortune. God meant us to grow strong, healthy, robust characters and personalities.

"The only justification, I believe, for our continued existence in this world is the privilege which we have of growing, of developing spirits capable of suffering, of sacrificing, and yet ever mounting."

She quoted from one of her favorite poets, Robert Browning:

When the fight begins within himself
A man's worth something,
God stoops over his head,
Satan looks up between his feet,
Both tug; he's left himself in the middle,
The soul awakes and grows.

She often referred to Browning. In a talk on stewardship she said this: "I like a thought which comes from Browning's 'Fra Lippo Lippi.' God has lent us great gifts to help save the world. I like the idea that our time, our talents, energy, personality and possessions are just lent to us by God and that we must return them to Him."

God uses us to help each other so,
Lending our minds out.

For the first seventeen years of her life, Annie Dove Denmark did her growing in her home in Goldsboro. She describes their evenings at home around the turn of the century.

"The lovely nickel lamp was lighted. Papa read his Sunday school lesson, and we children studied our school lessons. Mama often had ironing to do.

"Papa would open the wardrobe and get an apple or [an] orange and give each of us a section. At times other than Christmas each child had to be satisfied with a section of an orange or apple."

Annie Dove always remembered her sister's wedding because she played the wedding music. Her brother Walter said that he remembered the date, March 8, 1899, because on that day [for the first time in his life] he had a whole [whole] banana.

Walter was the middle brother. Fresh fruit and sweets were not so plentiful when the older Denmark children were growing up.

"I can remember my father reaching in his vest pocket to get out a penny for each child [as we went to Sunday School]. A penny was worth almost a dollar then," she said.

She recalls that when they got new fall shoes they kept the shoe boxes until Christmas to empty "Santa Claus" into. What they called "Santa Claus" consisted of one apple, one orange, English walnuts, raisins, French candy, and stick candy—lemon, hoarhound, and peppermint. There was no bubble gum!

Her oldest brother Edward would always save Christmas longer than anyone else. He would have his orange longer than the others and tease the other children after they had finished theirs.

Their mother cooked a cake every Saturday but at Christmas she cooked several. In those days before waxed paper she always put the cakes in towels in a chest drawer. The cakes were apple-jelly cakes, cakes with apple jelly between the layers. Miss Denmark said that when she was a child she did not know that there was any other kind of cake.

"My father always had a garden in which he took great pride," she remembers. Her mother canned tomatoes and other vegetables from the garden and made the apple-jelly which she used in the cakes. She remembers pig haslet or pork liver sausage as food she ate when a child.

"My daily task when I got home from school was to clean and fill the kerosene lamps," Miss Denmark reminisces. "I still have one of the nickel lamps. After Goldsboro put in electricity, Mother always had some kerosene lamps to be used in case of storm.

"I received my early education," Miss Denmark relates, "in the Goldsboro elementary and high schools, graduating in May, 1904. That was my first commencement."

"The schools which I attended had some very distinguished men as superintendents—Dr. J.Y. Joyner, for one, who later became state superintendent [of Public Education]. Dr. J.I. Faust, who became president of North Carolina College for Women [in Greensboro], was another. Several others also went on to presidencies."

Annie Dove was ten when she joined the Second Baptist Church, but one of her first remembered spiritual decisions came as a small child when she was washing dishes.

"My three brothers brought in the wood and mowed the yard, but I always had to wash dishes. I resented this and rebelled against having all the dishes to wash. One day I was looking out the window and I had a new spirit. I said to myself, 'What does it matter? It will soon be over.' I never minded washing dishes again."

Annie Dove Denmark says that she has had many spiritual experiences since this early remembered one. Now past eighty she believes that she is not a finished product.

"Life grows richer and deeper and sweeter as the physical curve dips and the spiritual curve rises—and that is as it should be," she affirms.

She heard the late Dr. Ellis Fuller, at the time he was pastor of the First Baptist Church in Atlanta, speak at the Ridgecrest Assembly, Ridgecrest, North Carolina. He said, "If I had my life to live over, I would major in the Holy Spirit." This inspired Miss Denmark to devote hours studying everything in the Bible about the Holy Spirit.

"Through a study of the Holy Spirit, I can grow spiritually. When the physical powers grow weaker, one must concentrate on the spiritual. Growth is the hallmark of health whether one is seventeen or seventy-five," Miss Denmark insists.

She wrote a friend, "You are an active person. I'm much more the slow, contemplative type, learning many new lessons late in life. That is as it should be for certainly there is no place for any one of us to ever stop learning either here or hereafter."

She likes the verse, "Because they have changes, therefore they fear not God," Psalms 55:19. She gave this paraphrase of the verse, "Because they have no changes, they are in trouble."

"There are three things I always strive to be," Miss Denmark quoted recently from one of her many small black notebooks, "a thoughtful learner, reverent student, and researcher."

Chapter 4

Music Wherever She Goes

I will praise the name of God with a song, and will magnify Him with thanksgiving.
—Psalms 49:30

Music was my first love," Miss Denmark told the Anderson College students in a chapel talk.

She emphasized that it is not just a blissful, sensuous experience. "Music is not only for the senses but for the mind and the spirit."

She often talked about music, which she called the most tangibly spiritual of all the arts, but warned that it could become the most dangerous. "Study of music can be of the highest and most intellectual value. Music is a language with a poetry as noble as that of a Dante or Racine. You are never too old to learn music. What we need is more music. We do not need so many more musicians. We need more listeners."

At the age of nine there was not much question about what career Annie Dove Denmark would follow. She was going to be a musician when she grew up. That was what she unhesitatingly told everyone.

When she talks of her early years in Goldsboro, she remembers the important role music played. She began the study of piano soon after she started to school, taking piano lessons from Mrs. Hiram L. Grant, who played the organ at the First Baptist Church.

When asked why she began the study of piano, she had this to say: "My parents wanted me to study so that I could play at church. I think when a child enjoys music and can have lessons, it is a deposit she can never get away from."

Students took part in programs at the college's on-campus radio studio. Pictured from left to right are 1952 students Rose Marie Creswell, Sarah Jo Johnson, Jerry Price and Helen Hendley. *Donated to the University Archives by the Hendley family.*

Her father, whom she adored, was proud of her accomplishment in piano. She and her father were always very close.

"As I look back, I remember how my father used to sit and listen to me practice by the hour," she said, "and on Sunday afternoons it was our custom to sing hymns while I served as accompanist.

"Papa bought a second-hand piano for $125. I remember how much he paid for it, for I thought that was something very special," she recalls. "Among the happiest memories of my childhood were the occasions when Papa walked with me from our home to the house of Mrs. Georgia Freeman for one of my piano recitals. Mama was busy looking after my brother Robert, four years younger than I, but Papa always went with me to the recitals."

At the age of nine she was playing the piano for Sunday school at the Second Baptist Church of Goldsboro. When she was eleven she played the music for her sister's marriage ceremony in their home. She had learned the Mendelssohn and Lohengrin wedding marches and played both while the bridal procession walked about six steps down the hall.

After the vows of her sister, Mary Clyde Denmark, and John R. Crawford were spoken, she provided music for the reception. She played "The Black Hawk Waltz" and played and sang "Polly Wants a Cracker." She still remembers the words:

Polly wants a cracker,
So they say.
Have you seen my parrot
With the plumage gay?

She has colors brilliant
Like the rainbow rare.
Polly is a treasure
But a source of care!

In September, 1904, a slim girl of seventeen with long blond hair, which her mother had always braided for her, entered Meredith College to study music. The college, then known as the Baptist University for Women, was located in downtown Raleigh, almost under the dome of the capitol, but there was a peaceful atmosphere about the school. Edward Charles Brewer, the first president, headed the college. [Dr. R.T. Vann?]

Popular novels at the time were those of Elinor Glynn. Hit tunes were "Red Wing" and "The Merry Widow."

Annie Dove served as president of the Philoreatian Literary Society in her senior year and was graduated in 1908. After her graduation she continued her study of piano at Meredith while beginning her career as a teacher at Buie's Creek.

In 1958 Miss Denmark returned to her Alma Mater on the fiftieth anniversary of her class. Out of a class of nineteen, fifteen were still living. Nine returned for the anniversary.

One person who did much to shape her career in music was missing at Meredith in 1958, the late Miss Grace Louise Cronkhite. Miss Cronkhite became her piano teacher in her sophomore year at Meredith. That she would continue to follow music as a career was settled when she began her study with Miss Cronkhite.[5]

This remarkable teacher was noted for her skill in developing in her pupils a sound technique and an unusual capacity for artistic interpretation. She often said that she found in Annie Dove Denmark an ideal pupil.

The years after the completion of her music course at Meredith were spent in teaching and in further study. For twenty years she studied and

Miss Grace Louise Cronkhite was Denmark's coworker and friend for many years. For more information, see endnote 5 and Appendix E.

taught piano, teaching the first year at Buie's Creek Academy (now Campbell College in Buie's Creek, North Carolina).[6] During this year she returned for lessons with Miss Cronkhite.

One of the pupils she remembers teaching at Buie's Creek was Bessie Campbell, daughter of J.A. Campbell, founder and president of the Academy and College until his death in 1934. This pupil, now Mrs. Edgar Lynch, was for many years a member of the music faculty of the college.

Annie Dove Denmark was a pupil of Raphael Joseffy in New York during the summer of 1909. The year 1916–1917 was spent in study in the Virgil Piano School in New York, where she was a pupil of Alberta Jonas. For many later summers she studied at Chautauqua Institute [Institution] in Chautauqua, New York.

She was a colleague of her former music teacher, Miss Cronkhite, in Tennessee College in Murfreesboro, Tennessee, and in Shorter College, Rome, Georgia. She taught harmony and piano in Shorter College for six years, 1910–1916.

As a piano teacher she went in 1917 to Anderson College, where she taught piano from 1917–1925. Miss Cronkhite had words of praise for her as a piano teacher:

"She was a clever piano teacher, because she had an almost uncanny knack of knowing just how to treat her students to get the best work from them and make them work for her...Miss Denmark is a music lover of genuine warmth and ability. Music is a language she understands and she imparts her knowledge of it with contagious enthusiasm."

In speaking of her early career, Miss Denmark had this to say, "I believe that the reason I studied to become a music teacher was because I felt so keenly the desire to be of service to others. Because I thought that in such a way I might bring pleasure to others, I planned a musical career. Then, too, my homelife had been one of culture, and my mother and father were both lovers of music, so I suppose it was only natural that I should have been so inclined to make it my work since I had had it all my life. I have always been deeply interested in music."

Miss Denmark turned a sharp corner in her life when she gave up music for college administrative work. No longer having time to devote to the teaching of music, she was no less ardent in her support of the art of music, both in the Anderson College curriculum and in contacts outside. Anderson is a music-loving city, and many of its musicians received all or part of their training at Anderson College.

Christmas messages received by Dr. Denmark reveal that the holiday season brings to many former students of Anderson College memories of their president seated at a piano in the dining hall where meals were served family style, playing beloved Christmas carols during the dinner hour. These alumni write that for them the strains of "O Come All Ye Faithful" and "O Holy Night" are associated not only with the joy of Christmas but with traditions of gracious living and beautiful music of vanished college days.

It was Miss Cronkhite, her college music teacher, who early saw that Miss Denmark's first love, music, was to be supplanted by a greater love. "Miss Denmark's interest in and love for people, which made it possible for her to sacrifice the profession of teaching, was early foreshadowed in her very first teaching at Buie's Creek Academy, the year after she graduated from Meredith College. Her work with students was never confined to teaching piano, but reached out into their religious activities," Miss Cronkhite observed.

"Her personal interest, always broad and centered more in the character of the person taught than upon some detail of technique, made her students love her and respond to her as few teachers inspire that feeling in their pupils. Although early in her career she gave up teaching music she still gives it an important place in her life."

"Music is everywhere in the world," Miss Denmark has said. She likes to quote from John Keats: "Heard melodies are sweet, but those unheard are sweeter."

She calls music a medicine for disorders. "Sacred music," she has said "inspires and energizes."

Chapter 5

"I'll Take the High Road"

But they that wait upon the Lord shall renew their strength; they shall mount up with wings as eagles; they shall run, and not be weary, and they shall walk, and not faint.
—Isaiah 40:31

Miss Denmark is fond of quoting from John Oxenham's poem "The High Way and the Low."

"We as human beings have the power to choose. When does one do the choosing of the high road or the low road?" As Miss Denmark asked Anderson College students this question, she reminded them that they were making choices every day. They had to make decisions, she told them, as to whether they would prepare their assignments or neglect them.

"Shall I face this duty or escape it? Shall I read a cheap, trashy story, or a good piece? Main Street by Sinclair Lewis is about cheap, tawdry, and stupid characters. People need to be interested in something besides 'keeping up with the Joneses,' having the latest model car or television set, or the latest scandal of the neighborhood. There is greater satisfaction in talking about great literature or good music. And every student decideth the way his soul shall go."

"What you as an individual student thinks and does and is today, matters tremendously," she frequently emphasized.

Her mother had held up high standards of behavior and her influence was shown in her daughter. She was disappointed in students or faculty members who did sloppy or slipshod work, but her great love and sympathy prevented her from being too severe.

A habit which Miss Denmark considers significant in the molding of her life was begun in high school.

"One of my first suggestions to Anderson College students," she often said, "is that they take notes. I began taking notes in high school. When I heard something inspiring and stimulating to me, I wrote it down to share with my parents. It is a great challenge, exciting and rewarding. It helps to increase vocabulary and conversational ability. Taking notes and making notebooks has been a passion of my life.

"We know what Jesus said only because some of his followers took notes—and what notetakers they were!" Miss Denmark reminded the students. "Socrates had his Plato. Jesus had his Matthew, Mark, Luke, and John. How wonderful for us that these men were so inspired by what Jesus said that they kept some of his sayings for us."

Dr. Denmark has a scrapbook which belonged to her mother. The scrapbook has in addition to letters and items of personal interest many clippings designed to strengthen the spiritual life. Perhaps the hobby of collecting the deeply spiritual thought, the beautiful phrase, the enduring truth, was suggested to her by her mother's habit.

Out of this hobby begun as a schoolgirl, Miss Denmark has acquired an impressive library of more than one hundred notebooks, typewritten, indexed, with tables of contents, arranged according to subject for easy reference providing a reservoir of information on any subject she might wish to discuss. During her twenty years of study at Chautauqua Institute, Lake Chautauqua, she made scrapbooks on art, science, religion, philosophy, and politics. Another scrapbook contains notes on the operas and concerts heard one winter in New York.

She has a set of notebooks, written in her clear, rounded handwriting filled with sermon notes by such men as Dr. John E. White, Dr. Ralph W. Sockman, Dr. Shailer Matthews, and Dr. Harry Emerson Fosdick.

New Year's Day, Mother's Day, Ash Wednesday, Good Friday, Easter, Thanksgiving, and Christmas are made richer in meaning for Miss Denmark because of a wealth of material about these special seasons. "Priceless anthologies" she calls her collections of notes and gems on a variety of subjects, such as "The Junior College," "Music," "Words," "The Tongue," "Motherhood," "Prayer," "Growth," "Health," "Death," and "The Holy Spirit." The notebook on the Holy Spirit lists a number of songs on this subject.

Miss Cronkhite, Miss Denmark's colleague for many years, said of Miss Denmark's hobby, "During all Miss Denmark's girlhood and mature life she

Throughout her life, Dr. Denmark kept notebooks, which she often gave to others. Notebooks pictured here are the property of the University Archives.

has been an ardent student of the Bible and religion. Her skill at notetaking in longhand has developed through a habit of years. Always intellectually keen and quick of comprehension, her notes taken from any lecturer comprehend the heart of the message. Her choice of diction has developed through this practice of taking notes so that her powers of speaking and her written addresses are always distinguished."

Many of Miss Denmark's notes were taken during the ten years when Dr. John E. White was leading chapel services for the students of Anderson College and preaching at the First Baptist Church of Anderson. From these notes she prepared the manuscript for a book, White Echoes, which was published in 1932 by the Sunday School Board of the Southern Baptist Convention.

"The investments in mind," Miss Denmark once told the college students in a chapel talk, "are those made in and through odd moments. How do you spend your leisure time?" she asked. "Do you spend moments in just talking aimlessly?"

Memorizing poetry or scripture passages is another form of investment which she urged the students to adopt, although she admitted that this was not a popular hobby. "Always, for example, have a stimulating book near at hand," she advised.

"I love memorizing," she said as she told of her musician friends, the late Mr. and Mrs. Crosby Adams of Montreat, North Carolina, who kept on growing culturally and spiritually until past ninety. She frequently cited Mr. Adams as an example of a man who proved that memorizing was possible at any age.

Miss Regina Cook Cowdrick was another person spoken of with admiration by Miss Denmark because of her achievements in memorizing. Miss Cowdrick, for many years head of the English Department of Anderson College, began to memorize poetry when she was threatened with the loss of her eyesight. As a result she was able to recite such long poems as Robert Browning's "Rabbi Ben Ezra" and "Saul" before near-blindness prohibited the reading from her favorite poet.[7]

During her years at Anderson College Miss Denmark devoted many of her evenings to the study of Dante, Browning, Carlyle, and other writers with Miss Cowdrick as her guide. They spent a year studying Dante's Divine Comedy and another studying Browning's The Ring and the Book. One of her faculty members said of her that she never saw anyone who read and studied so much, setting aside hours every day for reading and study.

A prized quotation of Miss Denmark's from The Ring and the Book comes from the Pope. "The points of the compass have not fluctuated, and the polestar is still shining and guiding upward."

In retirement Miss Denmark makes "pillow books" from her notes, books of quotations given to relatives or close friends when in the hospital. Other "pillow gifts" have been given as birthday presents to friends.

When asked after retirement to write editorials for the Anderson daily papers, she wrote to a friend, "I really am battling a real struggle in my heart—the privilege and opportunity (in these last years) to share and to serve." In declining the offer, she said, "My style is not journalistic but personal. It is a different technique to write for publication—not like speaking."

Among the early influences of Miss Denmark's life should be mentioned the attendance in 1919 at a Student Volunteer Convention in Des Moines, Iowa, the first one in six years. Until the First World War, these conventions were held every four years. Attending the convention with Miss Denmark were two Anderson College students, Lila Washington and Myra Anderson.

Something happened to Myra Anderson at that convention to make her certain of what she wanted to do with her life. Her training over, she went to Japan as a missionary. When war broke out she had to come home, but she could not stay away when the fighting was over. Only the illness which led to her death at last brought her home.

Miss Denmark still has in one of her little black notebooks some of the notes she took. Something happened to her at that convention, but her path was not then illumined as clearly as was Myra's. Yet she has always spoken of the convention as one of the influences that caused her to resolve to give her life in special Christian service.

Chapter 6

"Then Welcome Each Rebuff"

Be strong and of a good courage. Be not afraid—neither be thou discouraged. For the Lord thy God is with thee, whithersoever thou goest.
—Joshua 1:9

The glory and essence of life is struggle," Miss Denmark frequently said. "Life is constant effort and discipline.

"I am glad that I was at Anderson College during the difficult years," she affirmed many times. "I am not certain that I could have survived prosperity. I had a grand time during the depression."

Miss Denmark has credited her parents with influencing her in attitudes toward material things. "My parents were frugal but not wealthy. I remember my mother warning that nothing is a bargain if you don't need it.

"I grew up in Goldsboro when they didn't have sewerage, and I can remember when electricity was put in," she relates. "I remember hearing my mother say that she wouldn't mind giving up any other modern convenience if she could just keep the newly acquired screens. The screens in the parsonage of the First Baptist Church were about the first put in in Goldsboro."

During her first year of teaching at Buie's Creek Academy Miss Denmark no doubt learned lessons in thrift which aided her in developing into an executive admired for her business acumen.

She received the Artist's Diploma in piano from Meredith College in May, 1908. The following year she taught in Buie's Creek Academy and it was Buie's Creek Academy that she passed her twenty-first birthday.

"In those days when I was teaching music in the academy I was making all of $45.00 a month," she laughingly recalls. "Nine of those dollars I paid for board. I had my room in one house and took my meals at another. On cold winter mornings I had to get up and make my own fire, and I remember when I went out to the woodpile in the backyard for kindling I always kicked [kicked] out all the lightwood knots I could find. We had no electric lights then, either, and my light at night came from a kerosene lamp."

Miss Denmark has called her year at Buie's Creek one of the happiest in her life. "Of course we had not half the conveniences then that we have now," she admitted in speaking of those early years. "What we call necessities today were considered as luxuries, and when you worked you really worked. But as I look back over that year, I realize that it was when I was twenty-one and for the first time making my living 'by the sweat of my brow' that I was happy. I gained invaluable experience there at little Buie's Creek Academy. I might also add, that from that salary of $45.00 a month I saved enough along with the help my father gave me to go to New York and study the next summer. I even bought a piano while in New York."

At Buie's Creek Miss Denmark became well-acquainted with the Campbell family, a family of college leaders. She worked under the leadership of the founder and first president of Campbell College, the Reverend James Archibald Campbell. The two sons of the founder of Campbell College were at Wake Forest College while she was teaching at Buie's Creek. She observed at first hand the struggles and courage that kept small church-supported colleges alive. She and Carlyle later became college presidents in South Carolina, he at Coker College for eleven years and she at Anderson College. From Coker he returned to North Carolina where he served for more than a quarter of a century as president of Meredith College.[8]

Buie's Creek produced another college president, Leslie H. Campbell. This son of the founder served for more than half a century as teacher, dean, and president of the early Buie's Creek Academy and its successor, Campbell College. Before retiring in 1967 at the age of seventy-five, he led the college in its transition from a junior college to a senior college.

When Miss Denmark came to Anderson College in 1917, she was not yet thirty. The student body was small and there were few buildings. The Whyte House and the wings to the dormitories had not been built. The former was constructed during the Seventy-Five Million campaign. Dr. Elmer Francis Haight, who succeeded Dr. Denmark as sixth president, was able to build a new library out of capital funds contributed by the Baptist State Convention.[9]

It was not till the administration of Dr. John Edward Rouse, the seventh president, that new buildings began to go up all over the campus, a Student

This served as the dean of women's office during Miss Denmark's years in that position. This picture is located in a 1926 *Viewbook*.

Center-Gymnasium, a Men's dormitory, an infirmary, art and music building, and the Watkins Teaching Center.

The Boulevard on which the college is located was unpaved in 1917 and often deep in mud. Since the campus had not yet been landscaped, there were no beautiful terraces.

Miss Denmark had no illusions about the difficult situation she faced when she became president of a struggling church-supported college in 1928. "The men who turned down the presidency had more sense," she said, "than to take over responsibility for a college unendowed and with an indebtedness of $60,000."

Dr. Charles E. Burts of Newberry and his brother, Dr. R.C. Burts of Rock Hill, both hesitated and finally refused the responsibility.

The indebtedness of the college may sound like petty cash to today's big-business-men college presidents. For an inexperienced young woman, the indebtedness weighed heavier than the second mortgage on the old homestead.

In Miss Denmark's report to the trustees on May 28, 1928, she wrote: "If I told you the truth of one corner of my heart it would probably shock you—that I, even I, have moments of feeling it is impossible to carry the load here...I am now in the business. I have accepted the responsibility, and 'having put my hand to the plow,' I shall not yet turn back."

Miss Denmark also reminded the trustees that within the past decade the number of schools and colleges within the bounds of the Southern Baptist Convention had been reduced from 128 to 99. In 1928 when the foundations of the business world had begun to totter, old institutions were being wiped out overnight.

Resolved that Anderson College should not die, Dr. Denmark called for a study of the educational needs of the community. With Dr. White she had begun to study the idea of a junior college, a new thing in South Carolina.

In 1929 the decision was made to reorganize Anderson College as a junior college. The plan immediately met strong opposition. This was before the day of community colleges. The junior college had not become the popular institution it is today. Senior colleges, struggling to keep alive with empty beds in dormitories and vacant desks in classrooms, labeled the competing junior college an inferior educational institution. To the uninformed the image of the junior college was that of an immature, not-yet-arrived college.

Dr. Denmark liked to use the illustration of the four-leaf clovers and the three-leaf clovers. "Four-leaf clovers might represent our Phi Beta Kappa students and we are proud of them, but there are so many three-leaf clovers. Junior Colleges should be proud that they are educating a second crop of leaders."

That fall Miss Denmark came before the Baptist State Convention in Spartanburg and asked them to ratify the change to a junior college.

"South Carolina is crowded with senior colleges," she told the convention. "Not every student can go to college for four years and not every student can profit by four years in college. I see in the junior college a democratic institution for the young people of South Carolina. It can be a good thing for the future of the state just as it has been a good thing for other states."

The moderator of the convention suggested that opposition to a change in an institution from a senior college to a junior college often came from the alumnae. He inquired of Miss Denmark her opinion as to how the alumnae would accept the change. Miss Denmark asked Mrs. Olin D. Johnston (Gladys Atkinson, 1923) if she would be willing to express her feelings about Anderson College changing its status.[10]

Mrs. Johnston was aware of the hostile attitude of some of the alumnae toward the proposed change. Facing the large gathering, she pleaded for support of the junior college. "If Miss Denmark, the trustees, and faculty of Anderson College have the vision to pioneer in the junior college field, we should commend them for their courage and wish them godspeed. I received my bachelor's degree from Anderson College, but I am proud that my Alma Mater is pioneering in the junior college movement. The change is being made

Dr. Denmark is shaking hands with Gladys Atkinson Johnston, a 1923 alumna. Mrs. Johnston was loyal to her alma mater throughout her life. For more information, see endnote 10.

so that the college can do a superior and distinctive type of work. Anderson College wishes to do more than simply duplicate the work of other colleges."

After Miss Denmark and Mrs. Johnston had spoken, they waited anxiously for a response from the audience. They were uncertain how the vote would go. Cries were heard from the floor of the convention, "Question! Question! Question!"

When the votes were counted, the moderator pounded with his gavel, announcing, "The Ayes have it!" [Doak S. Campbell]

The vote was not a unanimous one, but Anderson College opened in September, 1930, as a junior college. Academic standards were kept high. Approval of the curriculum was secured from senior colleges and universities, and from the beginning graduates of the junior college transferred without loss of credit.

That fall there were boys as day students for the first time, six of them. But in 1932 the depression came and colleges throughout the country began closing their doors. Annual payments of interest had to be met on the indebtedness of $60,000. The mortgage creditors called for their money.

It looked as if the small, struggling college could not possibly survive. There was speculation in the city of Anderson as to how the thirty-two acre campus and college buildings would be used when the college closed its doors. Faculty members becoming uneasy about the future of the college began writing letters of inquiry to other colleges. Only by a miracle could the college open in September.

The following excerpts from a letter written by Miss Denmark to E.P. Vandiver[11] indicates the seriousness of the situation:

"You as trustee and as banker have been our dependence in the effort to finance Anderson College through the past critical years. In our recent effort to improve the financial condition of the college, other men have pursued policies contrary to your judgment. Up-to-date these methods have failed and the bonding company now forces the crisis upon us.

"As president of the college, I am appealing to you to lend yourself affirmatively to meet this situation as it now is but harder to handle than it has been and lead us out of it. I believe you have the magnanimity to put aside personal feelings and injustices, for the sake of the college and handle the situation with patience, tolerance, and such brilliancy of tact as it is possible for you to muster.

"You have shown that you have power over men in many ways—your handling of the Baraca Sunday school class.[12] Surely, our college is worth the service of these gifts which you possess. It is a challenge to your generosity, to your diplomacy and statesmanship. You are equal to this aspect of greatness."

Mr. Vandiver did lend his efforts to meet the crisis. A trustee committee visited the Hibernia Trust Company in New Orleans [Frank McGee, Sam Prince]. In 1932 the college was refinanced. Dr. A.L. Smethers, chairman of the board of trustees, and President Denmark called the faculty into special session.

Dr. Smethers spoke briefly but frankly, explaining about the indebtedness which required the payment of $3,600 annual interest. "We are in the midst of a depression," he said, "and denominational support has fallen off. We are helping as many students as possible to attend college but most of them need scholarship assistance. Payments on the mortgage are due as well as the interest.

"President Denmark thinks there is a way to keep the college open. Miss Denmark, will you tell the faculty about the one way which is now a possibility for us?"

Miss Denmark shared the depressing facts with the faculty. "The mortgage creditors have agreed to let us continue to operate the college if we can take care of the interest and begin to pay the installments on the mortgage. If enough of the faculty are willing to join me in working for whatever salary can be paid after the trust company is taken care of, we can keep the doors of Anderson College open. You will remember that when you became members of the Anderson College faculty, I welcomed you to both the joys and burdens of the college."

When Miss Denmark placed the fate of the college squarely on the faculty, they rallied to her plan and made it clear that they chose to keep it alive.

Miss Grace Louise Cronkhite, head of the music department, spoke first. "I joined the music department of Anderson College in 1917 at the same time that Miss Denmark did, and I want to stand by her just as long as she has faith that this college is filling a need."

The next speaker was Miss Regina Cook Cowdrick. In a letter which she had written earlier to Dr. Denmark, she had expressed her apprehension about the college. She had been tempted to accept a more secure position which had been offered her. She now announced her intention to remain. "I have been with the English Department since 1920 and I would like to stay to see this thing through. I have always believed that it isn't what happens to you that matters but what the thing that happens to you does to you."

Then Webb von Hasseln[13] spoke: "I have been a part of Anderson College since the beginning, and I would like to continue teaching French and Spanish and German as long as I can serve the college."

Dr. Olga V. Pruitt,[14] college physician, who had been associated with the college since its opening, voiced her hearty approval.

After this it sounded as if all the faculty members were trying to speak at once. Such exclamations as "You can count on me!" "I want to stay!" and "I believe in Anderson College!" were distinguishable.

Miss Denmark expressed her appreciation to the faculty. "You have indicated your desire to sacrifice for the cause of Christian education in Anderson College. You are majoring in things of permanent value—things which money cannot buy. You may receive five months salary instead of nine but you are rich. With such faith as yours Anderson College cannot fail. Our prospects are as bright as the promises of God."

The late Leon L. Rice, attorney and first judge of Anderson County Court, commented on this action of the faculty in his Founders' Day address of 1948. A former chairman of the board of trustees, he had made a careful study of the history of Anderson College.

Dr. Olga Pruitt served as the college physician and instructor of hygiene from 1913 to 1956. For more information, see Appendix C. Image is from 1944 *Columns*, page 12.

"The college operated from 1932 to 1939 on the generosity and spirit of service on the part of Miss Denmark and her fine faculty," he said. His address was published in an Anderson College bulletin and in the bulletin he listed the names of thirty-two faculty members and administrative officers, recording the conviction that their names "constitute an honor roll of the faithful."

In spite of the courage and faith that made it possible to keep the college alive, those days were often difficult. On April 3, 1938, this entry is found in one of Dr. Denmark's notebooks: "In January I had shingles, in February: flu...The school year has been unusually hard—what with servants, teachers, trustees (sick)—and the unrelenting tension of the financial burden. But with it all I have been very happy and thankful to God for his many mercies."

During the depression years Dr. Denmark became convinced that Anderson College, as a junior college, served a real need with its terminal secretarial courses. She believed that study should include vocational needs. But she envisioned for the students a training much broader than one which prepared them for jobs.

"Study is only a beginning, for the students are to be in large part the social, civic, and religious leaders of tomorrow. A primary function of a college is to train leaders—a body of people responding to those aspects which we call intellectual, cultural, and religious.

"'Education,' says Plato, 'consists in giving the body and soul all the perfection of which they are capable.'"

Ten years after Dr. Denmark became president, the debt which she had inherited was assumed by the General Board of the South Carolina Baptist convention and finally paid off by the convention and friends of the college in 1938 [$25,000 And. Friends, $25,000 Bap St Con]. In her financial report for the year 1939–1940, Miss Denmark expressed her gratitude. "For the first time since 1932 we have been able to pay the full nine months salaries to the faculty. That is an accomplishment so thrilling to me that I feel like old Simeon when he said, 'Mine eyes have seen the glory.'"

Two years after the Convention accepted Anderson College's junior college status, it approved the change of North Greenville from an academy to a junior college. Finally came the day when Dr. Denmark's proposal that the two junior colleges of South Carolina Baptists be given the security of a regular schedule of appropriations for current and capital needs was passed by the convention.

And it was on Founders' Day 1953, just before her retirement, that Dr. Denmark was able to announce that $985,000 had been ear-marked to Anderson College from the Baptists of South Carolina. Now she was ready for the retirement from the presidency that came at the close of the 1952–1953 session after twenty-five ["1/2"] years as college president. She was leaving to her successor a college free from debt and assured of continued support by the South Carolina Baptist Convention in a long-term capital-needs program.

Dr. Denmark has nourished no feelings of self-pity for those dark days of depression. She recently remarked to a former student, "The college is flourishing under the president, Dr. Rouse. I am not sorry that I was the president during those years of adversity. I am still thankful for the dedicated faculty. There is [the essence of] glory in sacrifice."

When she wrote to Dr. Rouse in 1967, congratulating him on the tenth anniversary of his presidency, she commented that a good parallel or difference in his tenure and hers was from the modern cafeteria and food service to the way she used to barter at the kitchen door with mountain men—tuition for their daughters in exchange for eggs, chickens, apples, and potatoes. She added this comment, "One man educated his daughter by selling us potato chips. Nevertheless, those were happy days!"

Chapter 7

"Be Careful What You Wish For"

Seek ye first the kingdom of God, and his righteousness; and all these things shall be added to you.
—Matthew 6:33

One of Miss Denmark's chapel talks contained the warning, "Be careful what you wish for when you are young [careful "when you are young what you wish for"]. When you are old you may [might] get it."

"Nobody loves children and babies more than I do," Miss Denmark asserts. "There have always been children in our home from the time my sister's oldest daughter, Berta Crawford, was born, October 2, 1904, to the present time, and I have always had a baby to love."

She quotes Calvin Coolidge as saying, "I wouldn't want to go to heaven if no children were there."

Anderson College alumni remember hearing her relate how William Lyon Phelps used to warn, "Be careful what you wish for [when you are young]; [when you are old] you may [might] get it."[15] She related how his wish was for books [and he had no money to buy books] and during a busy career of reading and criticism every mail brought new burdens of books. [Now when he was old every train, plane, ocean liner was bringing books to him because everybody who wrote a book wanted him to criticize.]

"The thing I wanted most in life when I was very young was a family. I wished for children, and now that I am old I find I have ten thousand foster children. I never married and had any babies of my own, but now I have all these foster children—former students and their families. God has done everything in the world to compensate me for not having children.

Anderson College at one time had a Preparatory Department. Here, Dr. Denmark awards Helen Hendley Donnell the Most Outstanding Member of the High School Class during her 1951 graduation. *Donated to the University Archives by the Hendley family.*

"It is the most interesting work in the world, this work with young people," Miss Denmark often observed during her years at Anderson College. "Many a time I have had a mother or father say to me, 'Miss Denmark, do the best you can with my daughter or son. All the hopes of my life are centered in that child.' I always had a mental reservation, however, that I could not do for the child what the parent, perhaps, failed to do in previous years."

She suffered under no disillusion that girls in her day were not rebellious.

"You can't make over girls," she said. "Some girls are so unruly they will not listen to reason. Many girls have traits that will lead to disaster in the future. You cannot change them, but you can modify them."

There was a time when colleges were small enough for the college president and faculty to know intimately all the students. In those days recruiting officers went into the homes and offered inducements to students to attract them. The students did the bargaining, not the colleges. The students also let the colleges do the waiting.

Students standing in long registration lines were unknown in early days in Anderson College. Students and faculty ate family style in a college dining hall instead of waiting in long cafeteria lines. The hand-picked students at Anderson College were not regarded as numbers but as individuals. To the college president each student was "some mother's heart and some father's pride."

Friends have observed that it seems strange that a woman so capable of great love never married. Sometimes the present has a way of bringing back the past, and Miss Denmark has admitted to close friends that she has thought of how things would have been different if she had made other choices.

Perhaps at those times when marriage was being considered other things pushed it aside. She had wanted a career in music first. Then the career in music changed to one in religious education. After that was begun, there was no turning back. She had to complete what she had started. Her college work was what she had chosen and she said that in carrying it out she found a rich and satisfying life.

To attempt to pigeonhole neatly all unmarried women is an unrewarding activity. Outward signs may indicate that a few know little emotional upheaval. Others appear to pass through brief periods of depression and then find life gloriously worthwhile because love was not confined to a small family circle.

Miss Denmark was frequently called upon to give talks on Mother's Day. She spoke to the Baraca class of more than one hundred men in the First Baptist Church of Anderson on the subject, "Motherhood."

"There are many women in the world who have given birth to children, and yet do not possess the noble qualities of motherhood. Conversely, there are some women, who, like Jane Addams[16] and Frances Willard,[17] have never given physical birth to children but have spent their lives making the world a better place for children." She pointed out that Anna M. Jarvis, the founder of Mother's Day, was childless.

Emphasizing the privileges and responsibilities of motherhood, she said, "The inspiration of my work as president of Anderson College lies in the realization that I am trying to make Anderson College girls more capable of becoming good mothers." She rejoices when one of her former students finds love and marriage. "I believe," she has said, "that as a general rule a girl should marry. Ordinarily her life is not complete without it. My life has been so full that I have not missed it, but this is no sign that I do not think the young woman of today should marry and have a home."

An Anderson College student, Ruby Crow, gave this description of Miss Denmark (Aunt Dovie) in a letter to a friend: "I think knowing her is like reading a book, a truly interesting one. Each day spent with her is a new chapter read, disclosing another angle of the personality which is being portrayed. I find so little that is extraordinary in the character portraits which my friends unconsciously draw of themselves. They invariably tell me the whole story in the first chapter—a story without individuality and color, in which they, as the main characters in the novel of their daily experiences, somehow remain always in the foreground. With Aunt Dovie it is different. One rarely ever has a glimpse of her real self because her horizon is so cluttered up with the lives and interests of other people."

Visitors to Miss Denmark's apartment at Anderson College often expressed their delight in viewing the beautiful Madonnas adoring the walls. She is quoted by one of her visitors as follows: "Yes, I know that art has reached its highest place and genius in the Madonnas, but my interest is not primarily from the point of view of art. I love my Madonnas because of the motherhood represented in them—a mother is creative and life-giving." She names among her favorites a Murillo "Immaculate Conception" and Raphael's "Sistine Madonna." "Music also," she hastens to add, "has not neglected mothers."

A former Anderson College student, Mrs. Jerry Price Bryant, remembered that collecting Madonnas was one of Dr. Denmark's hobbies. On a visit to her in Goldsboro she counted thirty-six Madonnas on the walls of her living room,

During her time at Anderson College, Dr. Denmark lived in the West Dormitory, now Denmark Hall. Here she sits in her campus apartment with Vera Lee Mulliken (left) and Betty Allison.

and she left taking some beautiful Madonna prints with her. Dr. Denmark possesses boxes of attractive Madonna Christmas cards.

"Dr. Denmark is a motherly woman," Reverend Charles Jollay, a retired minister, said of her. "When I was doing some work for her on her house at Ridgecrest, she put her hand on my shoulder as if I were a little boy."

It would be difficult to believe that a woman with great emotional power like Miss Denmark could have found life's richness through service to others without some moments of stress because of unfulfilled longings, of aching voids. Much of this can be only surmise. She does not bore others with descriptions of her own inner conflicts.

A teacher formerly associated with Dr. Denmark recalls hearing her in a rare moment of despondency speak of the seeming futility of repeating the same routine year after year. Always in a new college year before the days of population explosion there were the ever-recurring details—enlisting enough students to open the college doors, enrolling them, orienting them and encouraging the homesick students and their mothers to allow a little longer time for adjustments. All of this could grow as monotonous as cooking meals and washing dishes three times a day, year after year if one were not dealing with personalities with undying potentialities.

But no two girls are alike and no two years on a college campus are similar. An Anderson College faculty member once remarked that she would be glad when a certain year was over because a problem girl would not be returning. Dr. Denmark reminded her that other students with unattractive personality traits would replace her. Often she had occasion for rejoicing when disturbed students were helped to find healthy attitudes toward life.

One of these emotionally unstable adolescents disappointed her elderly parents and the college. She forsook her graduation plans for a clandestine marriage just before commencement. Several years later a letter came to Miss Denmark from the former student, expressing gratitude for all the college had done for her. The tone of the letter indicated that in spite of mistakes, transformation and happiness had grown out of a return to earlier teachings of parents and college.

"Young people and adults need warmth and tenderness," Miss Denmark has said. These she attempted to give to students and to others in the community for thirty-six years at Anderson. Today she does not have a family of devoted children and grandchildren of her own. But with a radiant smile she reveals that she loves and writes to and carries in prayer to her Heavenly Father hundreds of former Anderson College students and their children and grandchildren. And she affirms that love has been returned to her a hundredfold.

Chapter 8

"Are You Part of the Problem or Part of the Answer?"

For the Lord knoweth the way of the righteous; but the way of the ungodly shall perish.
—Psalm 1:6

Are you part of the problem or part of the answer?" Alumni remember hearing Dr. Denmark ask this question in a chapel talk. She said she believed it was the wish of ninety-eight per cent of the students to be part of the answer to the many problems besetting them.

When Miss Denmark served as dean of women in the antespace-traveling days, she met practically the same problems deans of women discuss today around their conference tables. Campuses in the twenties were spared traffic and parking headaches, but lining up one hundred girls with chaperones for a shopping trip into the city could well be considered grounds for a letter of resignation by one of today's student counselors. But this was just a minor detail in the life of a dean of women when Aunt Emma was a Co-ed, and green grew the ivy [when Miss Denmark was seeking to make it a brave new world on her college campus].

Church-supported colleges today have reduced chapel attendance to not more than one or two days a week, but has any college discovered a workable solution to the problem of chapel attendance? At Anderson College students abided willingly or reluctantly by chapel regulations for five days a week right up until Dr. Denmark resigned. Occasionally students voiced their complaints vociferously in canteen and dormitory buzz sessions. Others asserted that they looked forward to chapel periods. Some took notes and a few of these still write to Dr. Denmark to thank her for these chapel notes which they affirm have meant much to them through the years.

She discussed with the students in one of her chapel talks the purpose of the service:

"Anderson College stands for the spiritual side of our lives. The part of us which is not seen is the important part. We believe that our chapel service is important. Many of the most cherished memories of college days include some chapel program. This is the one time of day when we have a surcease from all other activities. No attempt is made here in coercing people into thinking or acting alike. God is with us in this chapel more really than we realize. Our chapel service seeks to provide for a community of worship. I am sure you have your established place and habit of worship. God is a spirit and He is here with us. True worship cannot be selfish."

Speaking before the Southern Association of Colleges for Women, Dr. Denmark referred to the changing student attitude toward chapel attendance.

"Let us take, for example, the matter of chapel attendance in college. Our situation in Anderson College may be taken as typical of many colleges. In recent years I have felt increasingly hesitant about inviting outside speakers. What is the matter? Do we sing the wrong hymns, read the wrong psalms, or have the wrong order of service? Suddenly this fall, there came a revealing flash, when I asked the students this question: 'How many of you have been accustomed to any sort of daily corporate expression of religion before you came to college? Are we trying to maintain a daily religious habit of college life irrelevant to your home life?' There was obvious confusion and embarrassment, and we found that there was not among the constituents of our college a single home where daily family prayers were a practice. Are we discovering, then, that the lack of interest in chapel attendance is but the manifestation of a deep-seated and far-reaching change in the status of the homes from which the students come?"

It is pleasant to imagine that dishonesty was unheard of in the days of the idyllic little Red Schoolhouse and for many years later. A few colleges today boast of an honor system which assures that a student's cheating on examinations is as unheard of as snow in summer. In other institutions, dedicated teachers are forced to admit that cheating on examinations is the "fly in the ointment" and the "blot on the scutcheon" in an otherwise satisfying career.

Anderson College sought to meet this problem by instituting an honor code which majored in rewarding good conduct rather than penalizing bad behavior. For many years the Student Government Association had functioned more upon the emphasis of punishing infractions of rules than upon the goal of developing personal integrity and character.

On February 8, 1944, the Society of the CollegiAnnes was organized as an auxiliary to the Student Government Association. The CollegiAnnes and Collegians for the male students were the self-governing members within the Student Government Association.

The name of Miss Claire Lucas,[18] psychology instructor and student counselor, was associated with this honor code. Dr. Denmark and Miss Lucas did not always see eye to eye concerning the amount of freedom to be allowed students. Dr. Denmark was of the opinion that junior college students and their parents expected much supervision in those days before permissiveness became a fashionable word. In a slightly modified form the new honor system worked well under the direction of Miss Lucas.

Many college students faithfully cling to their own code which forbids reporting classmates. Students breaking this code are stigmatized as tattle-tales or finks. An Anderson College student under the honor system did not report a dishonest student but, securing another witness if possible, he attempted to get the student to report himself. Failing in this the student summoned a court and the suspected student was tried by his classmates.

Claire Lucas worked as an instructor and student counselor from 1942 to 1953. For more information, see endnote 18.

An honor code student, not wishing to become involved, might refuse to carry out the required procedure. Students who acted conscientiously were sometimes persecuted by other students. No doubt guilty students frequently escaped punishment by denying their guilt.

But Dr. Denmark called the system salutary because it enlisted students in an enterprise in which they sought to solve their own problems. She pointed out that there is a great difference between student government and self-government, that is government by a group of students and the government of each student by himself.

College students did not form marches of protest when Dr. Denmark was a college president. But college campuses have never been free of gripers. College students, like disenchanted husbands, complained that the food was not like that their mothers cooked. Dr. Denmark tried to enlist the aid of the student in stopping criticism.

"Each student," she said, "is a living definition of Anderson College, the justification for the existence of the college." She told the students, "When you criticize your Alma Mater, you are criticizing yourself."

Even before the days of the so-called new morality, Dr. Denmark faced problems which continue to plague administrative officers. How much is a church-related college required to do for the student who is insensitive to ethical and spiritual matters before deciding that the student does not belong? What of the corrosive influence of such a student on her classmates? Where should one draw the line?

Anderson College did not admit any debate about a student known to be under the influence of alcohol or having alcoholic drinks in her possession while under the jurisdiction of the college. Such a student was subject to expulsion.

No one but a college president or dean can know of the emotional toll demanded when the necessity arises to place a long distance call to parents, advising them that the college can no longer assume responsibility for their daughter. For Dr. Denmark much of the tragedy in such a situation too often lay in the fact that the student was only partially to blame.

"Take the matter of drinking!" she told a group of educators. "In our day the people who used liquor were of doubtful standing. But now in this upside-down world, the use of liquor has become (in some circles) a badge of conventionality if not of respectability! The ramifications of these things are very far-reaching. We must carefully detach ourselves from the connotations of our own time, and make a desperate attempt to understand the connotations of the younger generation."

Dr. Denmark thus faced realistically the fact that colleges must take the students as they come to them from a large cross-section of the country and from overseas. The families out of which these students come have often been uprooted in their religious tendencies, she had discovered.

She expressed herself as believing that these students could be guided in finding solutions to their problems, with responsibility resting squarely on their leaders.

> *Our young people must develop the ability to face problems and to make decisions. We shall only be able to help them if our way is the best way, and if we make it so clearly the best way in our own living that the student will take it with the feelings that he has chosen it as his way. That our problems are difficult we cannot deny, for the great task today lies in the field of human accomplishment and character. But to say that the human heart and mind, capable of performing such miracles in electricity and in chemistry (which we have seen in our day) are incapable of performing miracles in the political, social, economic, and religious world, would simply not be logic. Science is never baffled by difficulties. We had better give up all of our modern conveniences invented by science than to fail to solve our human problems.*

Chapter 9

"Spires of Faith"

The Lord forbid it me, that I should give the inheritance of my fathers unto thee.
—I Kings 21:3b

It's a thrilling story, the story of Anderson College," Dr. Denmark said at an Anderson College Founders' Day program. "Every past was once a present and every present was once a future. Traditions are not hitching posts but guideposts."

Founders' Day, beginning with its first observance in 1929 [college not registered in State Dept.], was always a red letter day at Anderson College. The 1929 observance marked both the first official recognition of the founders and the inauguration of Miss Annie Dove Denmark as president of the college. The principal speaker on February 14, 1929, was the late Dr. Harry Clark of Furman University.[19]

Emphasizing the significance of the fact that Founders' Day comes on Valentine's Day, Miss Denmark said, "Truly Anderson College was conceived and born out of hearts of love."

A Valentine luncheon with lace-bordered hearts, red roses and carnations, a birthday cake with candles, all these become a part of the annual Founders' Day celebrations. Friends also brought birthday gifts, the idea being suggested by Chautauqua Institute's "Old First Night" with requests for gifts.

Each year the gifts were set aside for a designated need of the college. During the years of depression Miss Denmark called the gifts a godsend.

The Anderson newspapers announced on one of these early Founders' days that friends had decided to have a "shower" for the college. One newspaper article announced: "Some will bring canned goods. Many of these will come from the county; others will bring other necessities—all of which will help the college brave the elements in this time of storm."

Dr. Denmark recalls gifts in other years going for the purchase of curtains for the stage, for new equipment for the science department, for replacements in silver, china, chairs and tables for the dining hall.

One year birthday remembrances went to the library. Records show that that year gifts were valued at $1,000. But larger gifts were also recorded. On Founders' Day in 1946, the four daughters of Mr. and Mrs. Charles S. Sullivan, all graduates of Anderson College, established in memory of their parents the Charles S. Sullivan scholarship, endowed for $5,000.[20]

"The money donated on February 14 will be converted immediately into war bonds," Dr. Denmark stated on the thirty-second birthday in 1943.

Honoring the founders of the college was not for Dr. Denmark a perfunctory service to be performed because it was a duty. In a letter to alumni in 1950

This dress was worn by Dr. Denmark to many formal occasions at the college. It was donated by Dr. and Mrs. M.G. Delbridge to the University Archives.

she wrote: "It is always soul-stirring and heart-warming to pay honor to those 'who laid firm our school's foundation.'"

The college president included the whole community of Anderson as contributors to the foundation of Anderson College, pointing out that it was a community enterprise. But she said that community interest in Christian education had its beginning long before the charter for the present Anderson College was granted on February 14, 1911.

"There is certainly an intimate succession between Johnson Female Seminary[21] founded in 1847, Anderson Female Seminary founded in 1881, Anderson Female College founded in 1890, and the present Anderson College we see today," Dr. Denmark said at one Founders' Day program. "None of these schools were failures. They were stepping stones, spires of faith!"

She continued by saying, "Anderson College is a survival and at the same time a revival of Anderson's immortal and insatiate community spirit longing always for the best and the beautiful in life and learning. The lines were broken in history, but unbroken in spirit."

Dr. Denmark called Johnson Female Seminary the spiritual forerunner of Anderson College. "For the benefit of each generation of students we go far back into records of history," she said. She told about the eminent Rev. William Bullein Johnson,[22] first president of the antebellum institution, a pioneer in higher education for women.

She gave credit for many of the facts about this Baptist leader [To Mrs. Julia Webb von Haselen and to Mr. J.M. Paget for catalog—diploma—other relics] to E.P. Vandiver, Anderson banker and trustee of Anderson College, who served for two decades as moderator of the Saluda Baptist Association. Mr. Vandiver related that William Bullein Johnson was a precocious child who could read when four years old and studied Latin grammar before he was six. First taught by his mother and private tutors at his boyhood home in Georgetown, South Carolina, he did enter some schools but did not have the advantages of a college education.

Dr. Johnson was president of the Triennial Baptist Convention for three years, riding horseback to Philadelphia when he was elected. In 1845, following Johnson's plan, the Southern Baptist Convention was organized in Augusta, Georgia. He was the only man to serve as president of the General Baptist Missionary Convention and the Southern Baptist Convention, having a large part in the framing of the constitutions of the two bodies. He was one of nine men who formed the South Carolina Baptist Convention in 1821.

Dr. John E. White, Dr. Denmark's predecessor, also talked enthusiastically about Dr. Johnson, stating more than once that his name should stand at the top among the Baptists of the South as organizer, parliamentarian, and preacher.

Anderson College students were told that Dr. Johnson surrounded himself with strong teachers at Johnson Female Seminary which later was changed to Johnson Female University. He served as chancellor of Johnson Female University from 1853 to 1858.

Mrs. Mary E. Daniel, a lady from Maine, was one of the favorite teachers of Johnson Female Seminary. There is a story handed down of how she took the girls out to see a sunset and told them that after they left her she wanted them to look at the setting sun and remember her. William Wagstaff, an Englishmen who had been a soldier at the Battle of Waterloo, taught music at the seminary.

Dr. Johnson died on October 1, 1862. At the funeral the girls from the institution which he had founded preceded his casket to the First Baptist Church in Anderson where he was buried.

Dr. Denmark told of how this early institution was forced to close when the War Between the States came on, the buildings being used as a branch of the Confederate mint, and later as barracks for Northern soldiers. "Although there were years between 1847 and 1911 when there was no institution of higher education in Anderson, they were only brief interludes," she said. "The spirit of educational enterprise lived on in the community."

Dr. Denmark inaugurated another Chautauqua custom, that of the "Drooping of the Lilies," for use at each Founders' Day service. Those present slowly [lifted and] lowered handkerchiefs in remembrance of the institution's founders. Before this took place Dr. Denmark called the names of the incorporating trustees and the presidents who preceded her.

Dr. J.A. Chambliss was the first president but for only one year, 1912–1913, under a temporary arrangement. The first yearbook was dedicated to Dr. Chambliss, a retired Baptist minister from Plainsfield, New Jersey. He was a teacher of English and did not have executive duties.[23]

Then Dr. John Finley Vines, while serving as pastor of the First Baptist Church, was president for one year, 1913–1914. He came out to the college and conducted chapel services, but for the most part was president in name only according to a student of that year.

While Dr. Vines was president of the college, the girls were required to go to church. The Baptist girls went to the Baptist Church but could go to the Methodist church once a month. Dr. Vines and his wife taught the girls to live on a high plane and to work actively in their home churches.

Dr. Vines was born in Jonesboro, Tennessee, October 6, 1873. Ordained as a Baptist minister in 1899, he was graduated from the Southern Baptist

Seminary, Louisville, Kentucky, in 1902. He was pastor of the Central Baptist Church in Chattanooga, Tennessee, 1902–1905, and also served as pastor of the First Baptist Church in Roanoke, Virginia. His wife was president of the Virginia Woman's Missionary Union and taught parliamentary procedure to Women's clubs. Dr. Vines also served as vice president of the Home Mission Board of the Southern Baptist Convention.

After leaving Anderson College, Dr. Vines was engaged for a time in evangelistic work. In 1933 he held a revival in Bolivar, Missouri. Elaine Dunseth, a 1941 graduate of Anderson College, was one of fifty-seven who made a profession of faith during these services, and along with fifty-one others joined the church and was baptized.

Dr. James P. Kinard, the third president of Anderson College, was in office for two years 1914–1916. He had taught English at Winthrop College and returned to become the second president of Winthrop. He died in 1951, and Dr. Denmark and others from the college attended the funeral rites in Rock Hill. [We attended Dr. Johnson's funeral!]

Mrs. Kinard died as the result of a fire in Charlotte, North Carolina, on January 20, 1963, at the age of 91. Funeral services were held for her in Rock Hill and she was buried in Newberry. Mrs. Kinard studied at a Hawaiian University while in her late eighties. She was a graduate of George Peabody College and had taught at Winthrop College.

Dr. Kinard attended the Citadel and Johns Hopkins University. He returned to the Citadel as professor of English from 1913–1914. He was known as an affable and scholarly gentleman.

An Anderson College student of those early years had the impression that Dr. Kinard was shy. He used to say that he was a modest man. He taught sophomore English and was fond of Gray's "Elegy in a Country Churchyard." He gave this poem to his students to be memorized. He never touched Browning's poetry, saying that it would take a whole year. During the years that Dr. Kinard served as president, the college prospered.

Dr. John E. White, coming into office in 1916, remained until 1927. Like Dr. Vines he served as pastor of the First Baptist Church of Anderson while president of the college. By the prestige of his name and influence he pulled the college out of its financial difficulties for the time being and together with the Seventy-five Million campaign put it on its feet.[24]

But Dr. White was a long distance president. He lived a mile away, came to chapel three times a week when not out of town. The Sunday school class for the college girls met in the Baptist parsonage, a frame building at that time.

Students sitting in the loggia connecting Merritt and the West Dorm, or Denmark Hall. Photo is located in a 1918 *Viewbook.*

For Dr. Denmark, Founders' Day was not just a time to recount the history of the college and to honor the founders, but an occasion providing the opportunity to lead the thinking of the friends of the college of the future.

"Since one generation sows and another reaps, it is our task to preserve and perpetuate that which has been handed down to us," she told the Founders' Day audience. "My faith in Anderson College is fixed and unshakable. No matter what happens to Anderson College materially the spirit of the college is imperishable and indestructible. We need you, your loyalties, your prayers, your spirit, and your energies. Every one of us here today, therefore, has the opportunity to make a permanent investment which will be here till the end of time and beyond."

Dr. Denmark was succeeded in the presidency by Dr. Elmer Francis Haight. He came to Anderson College from Furman University where he had been chairman of the Department of Religion. He was recognized as a great teacher and preacher. By his own admission he was not a business man, and he was serving at a time when the administrating of a college was big business. During his years of service a new library was built and the former president's home was renovated. Many changes were made in faculty and staff.

Anderson College has had seven presidents, six men and one woman. John has been a favorite name for Anderson College presidents. The present executive bears the name John Edward Rouse. In 1967 he observed his tenth anniversary as president of the college.

Dr. Denmark has remarked that when changes were made by her successors in the presidency in the policies of the college she tried to keep in mind her words that traditions were not hitching posts but guideposts. She recalls that not every alumna was happy over the change made during her administration which led to the reorganization of the college to a junior college status.

She knew that there were citizens in Anderson who gave as a reason for not making large contributions to the local college the fact that a woman was serving as president, but she was not much disturbed by this awareness. After she had made her announcement concerning retirement, the faculty submitted a petition urging her to reconsider. She expressed herself as deeply moved by this action of the faculty, but now that she has seen her goal accomplished of winning firm assurance from the South Carolina Baptist Convention of substantial [$185,000 ear-marked] support for its institutions of higher education, including the two junior colleges, she held to her decision to retire.

She has taken advantage of the numerous opportunities to congratulate Dr. John Edward Rouse for the progress he has made since becoming head of the college. She has seen him secure full accreditation by the Southern Association of Colleges and Secondary Schools for Anderson College and also win the cooperation of the community in rallying behind the college as it had not done since the early days of the college founders.

When Dr. Rouse became the seventh president of the college, she said that she recognized that he had a difficult road ahead because the college was suffering from serious financial difficulties. But when the proposal was voiced to move Anderson College to Charleston, she commented, "It probably is just a bubble."

Because Dr. Rouse was not only a dedicated person but an excellent business man, her prophecy proved true. The friends of Anderson College in Anderson and throughout the state gave concrete evidence that they could adequately support a growing Anderson College and a new college in Charleston.[25]

Dr. Denmark laughingly recalls the time when Dr. Rouse was serving as a newly elected trustee of another South Carolina Baptist Junior College, North Greenville. The freshman trustee, zealous for the college which he represented, was presenting convincing proof at a conference that the needs of North Greenville College at that time were more urgent than those of the other colleges supported by the South Carolina Convention. In reminding Dr. Rouse of this occasion, Dr. Denmark said, "I am glad you are on our side now."

At a dedication service at the First Baptist Church in Goldsboro in 1960, Dr. Denmark gave some echoes from the past. She reminded the audience: "The victories of yesterday are but the paths of departure for something new tomorrow. Nothing is ended. Our march is always from victory to victory."

Chapter 10

"Deep Calleth Unto Deep"

Deep calleth unto deep at the noise of thy waterspouts: all thy waves and thy billows are gone over me.
—Psalm 42:7

When Miss Denmark came from North Carolina to South Carolina by way of Georgia, she was walking in the footsteps of a man she greatly admired, Dr. John Ellington White, also a native of North Carolina. Often she acknowledged her indebtedness to her predecessor in the presidency at Anderson College. After 1927, the students at the college, who never knew him, must have felt that they did because Miss Denmark so frequently used quotations from him in her chapel and radio talks.

She said that her anxiety was to keep some of his thoughts alive for future generations. She had found that his fertile mind and wonderful imagination gave out food—spiritual inspiration of lasting value. She called him a big man spiritually, well-loved, who left his influence on her. She insisted that he made of her a much greater leader than she could have been otherwise.

Thus it was only natural that she should call the book of sermons compiled from her own longhand notes taken from his sermons by the title, White Echoes.

He was born in Clayton, Johnson County, North Carolina, an adjoining county to Wayne County, where she was born. His father was a preacher and teacher. In 1886 John Ellington White entered Wake Forest College and earned his A.B. degree in 1890. In 1905 Wake Forest conferred on him an honorary D.D. degree. Baylor University also conferred on him an honorary D.D. degree.

Dr. John E. White was the college president from 1916 to 1927, a pastor of First Baptist Church and Dr. Denmark's predecessor. Photograph is located in the 1923 *Sororian*, page 17.

He went to Mars Hill College to teach and formed a sympathy with mountain people which never left him. He was married on October 12, 1892, to Miss Effie L. Guess of Cary, North Carolina. In the same year he was ordained to the ministry. His first pastorate was in Wilson, North Carolina, and then he went to Edenton from 1893 to 1895.

Miss Denmark had heard of him as a preacher. She also knew of his service as secretary of missions of the North Carolina Baptist Convention, a position which he held from 1896 until 1901. Some thought he was too young and inexperienced when he was elected to this position, but he soon won the people of North Carolina by his gifts as a speaker and by his warm personality.

His life seemed to go in cycles. In 1901 he went to the Second Baptist Church in Atlanta and was there fifteen years. Here he was brought into touch with the Home Mission Board, whose representative he had been in North Carolina. Next he was in Anderson as pastor of the First Baptist Church and president of the local college. Then he went back to Georgia. His name was being mentioned at that time for the presidency of Wake Forest College, but another man was offered the position [Dr. Frank P. Gaines].

In July, 1927, Dr. White left Anderson to become pastor of the First Baptist Church in Savannah. After his resignation as president of Anderson College, R.H. Holliday, business manager, was made acting president. Since he served only a brief interval before Miss Denmark was named president, she is usually considered the immediate successor of Dr. White, assuming the duties on January 1, 1928.

When Dr. White died in Savannah on July 21, 1931, his body was brought back to Anderson and buried in Silverbrook cemetery. Here his friends placed to his memory a stately granite shaft at his grave. But the book, White Echoes, became a living memorial, preserving much of his wisdom and philosophy for his friends and admirers.

In Georgia, Dr. White served as president of the Georgia Baptist Board of Education and was a trustee of Shorter College where Miss Denmark [for six years] taught piano and harmony. He was responsible for inviting her to Anderson College where he appointed her dean of women in 1925.

In Anderson he threw himself with zeal into the work of the church, the college, and the civic life of the community. He tied in the college with the church, because he believed that "We belong to each other."

At the beginning of the presidency of Dr. White in 1916, additions were made to the dormitories, and another building was constructed to provide for an enlarged student body which reached 291. The college was in debt and a loan of $60,000 was secured from the Hibernia Trust Company in New Orleans.

He was a statesman and much interested in public questions of both state and church. He was known as a platform orator and was concerned with the importance of public speaking. Former students and faculty remembered his chapel talks on a favorite poet, Sidney Lanier.

During his presidency at Anderson College, Dr. White was not interested in seeing the college admitted into the Southern Association of Colleges and Secondary Schools. He considered that certain accreditation standards of the Association in those earlier years could hamper a college in its endeavors to do a distinctive work. Perhaps his attitude had some influence on Dr. Denmark. At least she never became greatly disturbed during the years of struggle when the lack of endowment kept the college out of the Southern Association.

The late Dr. E.W. Sikes, for many years president of Clemson College (now Clemson University) gave this account of a Southern Association meeting in Birmingham: "Luther at the Diet of Worms never showed more courage than did Dr. White when he stood before the Southern Association of Colleges in Birmingham and told them their standards were wrong. The body disagreed with him; he knew it; they knew it; but they showed their appreciation of his courage by rounds of applause."

Miss Denmark recalls a bit of conversation at the time that her father was introduced by the Rev. C.V. Brooks to Dr. White.

"This is Brother Denmark. He is just the salt of the earth," Mr. Brooks said.

"I can understand that," Dr. White quickly replied, "I've got a pinch of that salt down in South Carolina."

This photograph of Dr. Denmark comes from the 1928 *Sororian*, page 17.

Speaking to the students at the opening chapel service after she was made dean of women, Miss Denmark said, "Dr. White teases me sometimes and says he is making a preacher out of me. Maybe he is. I don't know."

At any rate his mantle fell upon her as she succeeded him as president of Anderson College. She remembers his saying that when God needed a leader he reached down and picked Him a man. But it was a woman who was picked to follow Dr. White.

On special occasions her thoughts seemed naturally to turn to words spoken by Dr. White. In giving a charge to a group of honor students, she said, "Dr. White used to talk to us about the soul and spirit of Anderson College. We sing our Alma Mater, "Truest devotion till life is ended / Always we pledge to thee."[26] But what is the spirit of Anderson College of which Dr. White was speaking? This too is Anderson College, the way you act, the manner in which you speak, your attitude toward faculty and other students."

Or again she referred to her former mentor in a challenge to the students. "I remember Dr. White saying, 'God needs you as much as you need Him.' He cannot make the world better except as he makes you better. He needs you."

"A bit quaint!" That could very well be the way one of today's students would describe a statement in the historical notes of earlier Anderson College catalogs. "The college was founded as a community enterprise, but its builders were not inspired solely by local pride; they felt the need of combating the influence of materialism upon the life of a little town fast becoming modern."

Dr. Denmark recognized the language as being that of Dr. White and she had the sentence copied for all the catalogs published during her administration. She called it a worthy goal, this ideal of Dr. White's to set alongside "the influence of materialism and industrialism" the beauty and immortality of music, the "best that has been thought and said" in great literature, the upward pull of undying spiritual truths.

Dr. Denmark recalls Dr. White speaking about the young people of his day. He said that critics referred to them as being in confusion, in revolt, but he believed that the young people of his day were no worse than they had ever been. "The trouble is that parents are not as good. If parents were as good as they wanted their children to be, what a wonderful world we would have," he said.

Serving as president of Southern Association of Colleges for Women, Dr. Denmark centered the program around problems of the young people of her generation when she addressed the group in annual convention in Louisville, Kentucky. Although panel discussions were not as well-known in 1935 as they are today, she had planned a panel discussion on the ambitious subject,

"Toward an Understanding of the Younger Generation." Dr. Frank P. Graham, at that time president of the University of North Carolina, had been secured as leader of another panel discussion on the subject, "How Youth Looks at Social and Political Questions." [no.]

Dr. Denmark has had ample opportunity in her career to observe the younger generation, but some of her remarks in opening the discussion seemed to echo the philosophy of her beloved Dr. White.

"I believe in the boys and girls of this generation, and it is the keenest joy to make my humble contribution to their specific problems," she said. "If they can't do a better job of their world than we have done with ours then I'm sorry for the world and the future is dark. I believe that our work with youth should be cynpathetic rather than critical. Direction is better than dictation."

In the preface to her book, <u>White Echoes</u>, Miss Denmark expressed her hope that the book would present to readers "the fresh and forceful thinking of Dr. White." She wrote, "My earnest desire is to pass on to others some faint reflections from that beautiful spirit who has so recently achieved the 'great adventure'...More than a hundred such sermons as these in this volume lie in my notebooks...I took them down in longhand as fully as I was able.

"They were Dr. White's sermons in basic structure and outline, but I have added from my own and others' thoughts what was needed to make them intelligible and coherent."

She noted that Dr. White had corrected and annotated several of the sermons, but his speaking was extemporaneous. She also reminded the readers that cold print could never "reproduce the electric quality of Dr. White's sermons."

Dr. White commented on her notebooks as follows: "Without shorthand she has reproduced my sermons in perfect manuscript, written out in her own hand. The striking fact about these manuscripts is that she was not a mere copyist, but an editor, so that sermons from her hand are very much better productions of thought and of English than they were from my lips." [Dr. E.M. Poteat said!!]

The late Dr. W.J. McGlothlin, who served for a number of years as president of Furman University, wrote the introduction for <u>White Echoes</u>. He called Dr. White "a thinker in constant touch with the religious, social, and political thought of his time, and a speaker of rare power." According to Dr. McGlothlin the sermons of Dr. White contained a "breadth and reach and power." He wrote that in these sermons "there was a profound sympathy with the deepest and best in man which gave to his preaching peculiar power, especially with the more cultured and thoughtful of his congregations."

Dr. Denmark calls typical of the spiritual reach and power of Dr. White the following words which she reproduced from one of his sermons in White Echoes:

> *We are conscious in a sense, that we do not belong in this world... We were created with the feeling in us that we are not fitted and prepared to occupy this world permanently. None of us is made to stay here long. The deep calleth us on as a great ocean calls...Do you ever get tired of the "here" of work, of making money, realizing the futility of it all? Life is only temporary and probational. You are only half-man until you find your other half, your better half, in the Father's spirit.*

Chapter II

"Whose Daughter Art Thou?"

Whose daughter art thou? Tell me, I pray thee.
—Genesis 24:23

Whose daughter art thou?" This was the searching question Dr. Denmark chose to discuss at one of the last chapel talks of the college year.

In Genesis the story is told of Abraham's servant Eleazer seeking a wife for his master's son, Isaac. "Abraham's interest in character and family was no different from that of parents today," the speaker said. "Heretofore you were the daughter of your parents only. You now belong to two institutions—your family and your college.

[Talking of the integration of faculty and students on a small college campus, she continued,] "A girl cannot live on the Anderson College campus and be the same girl she was when she came," Dr. Denmark continued. [mark out Dr. Denmark continued] "You are the Anderson College spirit. Anderson College is the sum total of the faculty and the students. Anderson College needs you even as you have needed Anderson College this year.

"What then is Anderson College? If Anderson College is the sum total of the faculty and students, its story is much too long to be told in any book." Here are the stories of just a few of those students from Dr. Denmark's treasury of precious memories.

Miss Denmark remembers Gladys Atkinson of the senior college class of 1923 as an alumna who made her schoolgirl dreams come true. Sitting in one of the picturesque wooden swings on the college campus, Gladys boasted to her classmates that she was going to marry a man who would become the governor of South Carolina. Since her home was in Georgia at that time, she must have already picked out the South Carolina man whom she planned to assist to the governor's chair.

Not long after receiving her A.B. degree she became the bride of Olin D. Johnston, a native of Honea Path, and former textile worker. She could claim a part in changing dreams into reality, for she served in her husband's campaign headquarters each time he sought and won the governorship of South Carolina and was his assistant when he was a candidate for the United States senate.

Miss Denmark testifies that Gladys Atkinson Johnston never forgot that she was a daughter of Anderson College. She served for more than fifteen years as a member of the college's Board of Trustees. When some of the senior college graduates lost interest in their Alma Mater because it had become a junior college she praised the move. One summer she spent long, hot afternoons accompanying Miss Denmark in house-to-house canvassing of prospective college students in her home city of Spartanburg. In days of depression when explosive college enrollments were as unheard of as atom bombs, the efforts of loyal alumnae helped to fill dormitory rooms and keep colleges alive.

During her years at Anderson College Miss Denmark was the only woman in South Carolina serving as president of a college. In her letters answering inquiries from parents or students she reflected her joy in her chosen work by writing, "It is my privilege to mother every student who comes to Anderson College."

Dora Hancock of Donalds wrote for a college catalog and received first a letter from the college president and then a visit from a member of the recruiting staff.

The college representative was a little [somewhat] abashed when she arrived at the home in Donalds and met an attractive young woman who could have been in her late thirties. Dora laughed and remarked [Laughingly Dora said] that she imagined Dr. Denmark would be a little startled at the idea of mothering a girl as old as she was, a girl who had worked in a textile plant for a number of years.

Dora became a daughter of Anderson College in 1950. "Although I realized," she said, "that I would be living in a dormitory where the regulations were designed for young teenagers, and I had been making my own way since graduation from high school in 1929, I resolved that I would see the thing through until I held my junior college diploma in my hand."

Because Dora was more mature than most freshmen, Dr. Denmark and others expressed concern as to how she would adjust to college life. She not only liked the college, rules and all, right off, but the other students admired her as evidenced by her election, first, to the presidency of the

Dora Hancock was an Anderson College student who returned to work at her alma mater. This photograph comes from the 1952 *Columns*, page 17.

freshman class, next, to a position as freshman representative on the Student Government Association, and in her sophomore year, to the presidency of the Association.

After graduation from Anderson College and further study at a senior college and at Southwestern Theological Seminary, Dora returned to Anderson College as a member of the faculty and adviser in religious activities. Her Christmas greetings to those who made it possible for her to secure a college education always bear these words, "Thank you for being my friend."

Dr. Denmark vividly remembers another student whose dreams came true. In the beginning an ambitious and loving mother did most of the daydreaming. But in the end after years of study and struggle, disappointment and tragedy, the former Anderson College student realized the early dreams that the two of them had fashioned.

Anne Jeffreys Carmichael was born in Goldsboro, Miss Denmark's home town. When Anne was fifteen, her mother brought the tall blond daughter to enroll her in the Preparatory Department of Anderson College. Seated in Miss Denmark's living room, Mrs. Carmichael told her former Goldsboro neighbor that her ultimate goal for Anne was a career as an opera singer. So Anne studied for a [that] year with Miss Katharine Culyer as her teacher. Miss Denmark may have smiled at the mother's extravagant hopes for her daughter, but following her career with interest, she always remembered Anne's singing ability and her striking beauty.

Departing from Anderson, Anne made her way to New York City where voice lessons were financed by work as a model. She tried a number of jobs to earn a living, memorizing operatic airs in preparation for the big opportunity which never came.

Then she went to Hollywood where her name was shortened to Anne Jeffreys. Movie goers know the rest of the story. She made her movie debut in 1942 in "I Married an Angel," singing with Nelson Eddy. Then came her later successes, including the lead in "Kiss Me, Kate."

But few persons know of the part that her devoted mother played in her success. Anne revealed something of this in a letter to Dr. Denmark after the death of her mother. Mrs. Carmichael never lost faith in her daughter's ability to make a success of a singing career. She it was who encouraged her through the difficult years in New York.

Mrs. Carmichael not only devoted her life to her daughter, but Anne's son is alive today because his grandmother saved him from death beneath the wheels of an automobile whose brakes failed. The grandmother lost her life but not before she had snatched the little boy from beneath the automobile that killed her is it rolled backward down an incline.

During her years as a college president, Miss Denmark came to know many mothers who did without the things they needed to enable daughters or sons to attend college. For Miss Denmark, Mrs. Carmichael became symbolic of this mother who would willingly give her life for her child or her grandchild.

In a letter sent to senior and junior graduates and graduates of the Preparatory Department Dr. Denmark addressed alumni as sons and daughters of the college. She has said that this is the way she always thinks of them.

"The greatest source of joy which I have in Anderson College and the one source which will abide forever is the realization of loyalty and devotion which I know exists among Anderson College girls and boys everywhere the world over. You have a pride in the fact that you are known not only as sons and daughters of your parents, but also as sons and daughters of your Alma Mater—Anderson College."

More recently Dr. Denmark has appealed to this loyalty of the sons and daughters of Anderson College as she has heartily endorsed the Living Endowment plan.

"Support of the Living Endowment fund makes you a partner with the founders and the friends of Anderson College who have contributed large and small gifts through the years. We must not forget that more is spent on each student than is received from him in tuition and fees. Church-related colleges must depend on loyal alumni and friends to invest money regularly in the great enterprise of training our youth."

["My daughter wouldn't then be all fair?"]

Chapter 12

"I Have Called You Friends"

No longer do I call you servants—but I have called you friends.
—John 15:15

In one of her chapel talks Miss Denmark insisted that no human relationship could be considered complete until it is crowned with friendship. She called tenderness and devotion the ingredients of friendship. "And then how true it is," she continued, "that friendship often becomes the indispensable and sustaining power without which at times we could not go on."

"Teacher and disciple, that is not enough," she asserted. "Lord and servant, that is not enough. Nothing is enough until one can say, 'I have called you friends.'

"Then let us magnify our friendships. Let us be worthy of our friends. Let us be true to our trusts and keep ourselves free from littleness of thought and motive and deed. Let us remember always that 'there is a friend that sticketh closer than a brother.' We Christians know who this Friend is, even Jesus our Lord. To have Him as our Friend is to be rich, indeed."

Artists presenting programs, speakers for Religious Emphasis Weeks, parents or relatives of students, business men and women—these came to Anderson College as comparative strangers and went away as friends of the college and of its president.

Every member of the Women's Missionary Union of the Southern Baptist Convention knows about Miss Fannie E.S. Heck, who served three different times as president of the Union. She is the author of Royal Service, history of the first twenty-five years of Women's Missionary Union and of the Woman's hymn, "Come Women, Wide Proclaim."

But Annie Dove Denmark claims her as her friend and Sunday school teacher. She is often called upon to tell the story of Miss Heck's life at society or circle meetings.

In giving the commencement address at the WMU Training School in Louisville, Kentucky, in 1940, Dr. Denmark said, "I thank God that I knew personally Miss Heck during the years 1904–1908 while I was a student in Meredith College. I was in her home in Raleigh on various occasions and knew something then of the radius of her life...She was one of those great souls whose high courage and ideals will continue to illuminate the lives of the procession of young women who come here, to quicken them in the expanse of their own lives."

Miss Denmark has always demonstrated a tender love for people in their sunset years—women whose eyes hold a wistful look when talking of the long ago and who smile gratefully when love and attention are proffered them. As a young music teacher in Anderson she manifested that love and interest by teaching a class of older women in the First Baptist Church.

Miss Denmark's friendship with the musicians, Mr. and Mrs. Crosby Adams, began when they were approaching their eighties and living in "the House in the Woods" in Montreat, North Carolina. It was on March 25, 1937, that Mrs. Adams first came to Anderson College for a piano recital on her seventy-ninth birthday. Each year after that the pilgrimage became an annual event.

On one of those annual visits Mr. Adams recited two groups of poems to the Anderson College faculty. At the age of ninety he took up the hobby of memorizing poetry and prose passages.

At her ninetieth birthday recital Mrs. Adams announced her piano selections in a voice that penetrated far back under the balcony of the college auditorium. The college students and guests from Asheville, Atlanta, and other cities applauded enthusiastically the program of fairy-like music produced by the fragile little woman with the merry twinkle in her blue eyes and the soft smile upon her lips. The children in the audience forgot their usual restiveness and only the March wind in the pines near the windows broke the stillness as it accompanied the playing of Mrs. Adams's own composition, "The Aeolian Harp."

"Can life still be interesting when one has lived beyond the threescore years and ten?" asks the septuagenarian. For many people in the audience Miss Denmark had supplied the answer to that question by bringing Mr. and Mrs. Adams to Anderson College for a recital by Mrs. Adams on her ninetieth birthday.

When counting "Life's Extras" Dr. Denmark always mentions her association with genial Dr. Charles D. Johnson of Baylor University.[27] She knew him during many of the twenty-one years that he was serving as chairman of the Education Commission of the Southern Baptist Convention. He frequently called on her for articles for the two publications of the Commission which he founded and edited for fifteen years.

During a number of those years the annual meetings of the Education Commission were held at Ridgecrest. Dr. Denmark remembers Dr. Johnson's efficiency as a presiding officer. But she remembers best of all his infectious laughter at some of the jokes told about college deans and presidents.

Dr. Johnson evidently considered that meeting a near-failure that did not have a woman college president on the program. At least he placed Dr. Denmark on the program as often as he could persuade her to participate. Others appearing often on the programs were Dr. Hoyt Blackwell, president of Mars Hill College; Dr. Spright Dowell, president of Mercer University;[28] and Dr. Doak S. Campbell, president of Florida State University. Dr. Denmark also noted that every time her name was on the program the name of Dr. Lawrence T. Lowrey, president of Blue Mountain College,[29] also appeared. They seemed to be the two that Dr. Johnson always turned to when he needed speakers.

One summer Dr. Denmark was relaxing at Ridgecrest. She was not working on a speech and was looking forward to the program when she would be free to listen and would not have to assume any responsibility.

Congratulating herself on her freedom, she looked out the window of her summer cottage, Cragamo, and saw Dr. Johnson almost running up the hill from the auditorium. Some one had disappointed him at the last minute and he must have a speaker to pinchhit for the missing guest.

Had we but time enough many thrilling stories of friendships could be resurrected. How could one begin to record the names of friends from Anderson? But no Andersonian would expect to find the name of the birthday lady omitted—Mrs. J.M. Paget. During Dr. Denmark's years in Anderson, Mrs. Paget never forgot to send her a note and perhaps some homemade cake, orange marmalade, pear relish, or scuppernong jelly. On one of the notes she wrote, "My time is full to overflowing with home life and duties and business cares and teaching a Sunday school class of seventy-five young matrons and looking after my Birthday Family of around two thousand. I am convinced that attending to my birthdays is my big work that God means for me, and I get a world of happiness from it."

On Dr. Denmark's fiftieth birthday the birthday lady wrote to her and it was almost like a page out of Browning: "I want to tell you that I think fifty the most splendid and glorious year of a woman's life, and I consider as I look back, my time between fifty and sixty my golden age. Judgment is more mature; much experience has brought wisdom and understanding; the heart grows tenderer, sympathies broaden, outlook on all of life is widened... It is a beautiful thing to me to look back through the years since you came to Anderson and watch your growth. No difficulty has stunted it because of your sublime faith."

Operating a college is a matter of teamwork and there would be no stopping place if one tried to name all the friends in Anderson. But it should be mentioned that Anderson College has a trustee emeritus or life trustee as well as a president emeritus. Dr. Archie L. Smethers said that he could hardly remember when he was not serving as chairman of the Board of Trustees of the college. He served during all the time that Dr. Denmark was president and played a major role in tiding the college through critical periods. But the saga of this Anderson physician and civic leader and his lovely wife and their dedicated service to Christian education is still another story.

Dr. Denmark revealed her belief in the close relationship between churches and colleges in her opening remarks in each baccalaureate service held in the First Baptist Church. These were her oft-quoted words: "In the records of the [old] First Baptist Church in America founded by Roger Williams in Providence, Rhode Island, in 1638 there is a quaint entry which reads 'a

This billboard is pictured in the 1943 *Columns*, page 36.

Meeting House for the Public Worship of Almighty God and also for holding Commencement in.'"

Pastors from the different denominations in Anderson brought their greetings to the students at the Anderson College opening convocations each year and were frequently heard at chapel services. Two of the presidents of Anderson College were concurrently pastors of the First Baptist Church, Dr. John F. Vines and Dr. John E. White. Another pastor of the church, Dr. Cort Flint, served as acting president for a short time after Dr. Elmer Francis Haight resigned to become a member of the faculty of Louisiana College and before Dr. J.E. Rouse was elected.

Dr. Denmark has said that she felt at times that the personnel of the Anderson newspapers, their editors, reporters, and photographers were all a part of the larger staff of Anderson College. One school of thought insists that a college must have winning athletic teams to secure wide publicity. Because of the interest of the Anderson newspapers and their publisher, Wilton E. Hall, in Christian education, Anderson College was enabled to disprove this theory. Dr. Denmark often emphasized that it would be difficult to evaluate the contributions made to the college over the years through the local newspapers and radio and TV.

Just as it is difficult to name the founders of Anderson College since the whole community is included, so it is an unending task to enumerate the friends of the college. Nowhere is teamwork more necessary than in keeping a college in the forefront of service. Dr. Denmark sees a wonderful example of that teamwork moving in behalf of the college today in the launching during Dr. Rouse's administration of the Living Endowment movement.

Chapter 13

"Stay Away from Where You Have Been"

The place whereon thou standest is holy ground.
—Exodus 3:5

Dr. Denmark admits that she had her misgivings in retiring from her position as president of Anderson College in June, 1953. She realized that many retired persons have difficulty in adjusting to free time stretching out into a seemingly endless future.

She said that she would miss the association with young, inquiring minds. She has often quoted the warning she heard Dr. William Lyon Phelps make at Chautauqua, "If you want to stay young, associate with young people; but if you want to die young, try to keep up with them."

She had her doubts in returning to her childhood home in Goldsboro, North Carolina. Since 1917 Anderson College had been her home. She had lived in the atmosphere of a church-related college for thirty-seven years at Anderson College, in addition to short periods spent as piano teacher in schools in North Carolina, Tennessee, and Georgia.

For twenty-six years she had held the highest executive position at Anderson College. As the president of the college, she could expect plans she initiated to be carried out. Accustomed to having many persons to look to her for guidance, she was often buoyed up by a feeling that she was filling a need.

She would be beginning an entirely new way of life. At a college commencement she commented, "For more than a third of a century it has been an unbroken annual occurrence for me to be present in some college commencement exercise, and often in two or three commencements during the same year."

This picture was taken at Dr. Denmark's retirement in 1953. Family members in attendance are (from left to right) Virginia Crawford Henderson, Robert Denmark, Dr. Denmark, Willis Denmark, William (Bill) Denmark, John R. Crawford Jr. and Edward Denmark Jr. *Courtesy of the Denmark family.*

Friends expressed anxiety at any decision causing too complete a break with the past. Devoted admirers in Anderson urged that she make her home in the city where she had labored so long. At their insistence she looked at one or two possible home sites. Driving around Anderson she thought nostalgically of happy hours spent with friends. She remembered challenging early struggles, festive occasions, and heart-warming deeds of kindness by loyal citizens.

All through the period of transition Miss Denmark had an intuition that, much as she loved Anderson, she should not be swayed by emotion in making her decision. She quoted Charles Wesley as saying [to young Methodist ministers], "Go where you are sent and stay away from where you have been."

When the time came to give up the presidency of Anderson College, she had completed her plans to make her home in Goldsboro. A large, rambling, one-story house two blocks from Main Street was remodeled as a home for her and three other former teachers of Anderson College.[30]

During the early weeks of retirement she read Anderson newspapers page by page. Letters from Anderson friends were eagerly anticipated. Information from Anderson was top news value to her.

Then Miss Grace Louise Cronkhite became ill. She was the former chairman of the music department at Anderson College and had accompanied Miss Denmark to Goldsboro. Until her retirement in her eighties, Miss Cronkhite had been sought by Anderson's most talented music pupils. Now that her teaching days were over, her health gradually failed.

Older people have a special place in Miss Denmark's affections. Among her happiest memories are those connected with the Sunday school class of women, ranging in age from fifty to ninety, that she taught when she first went to Anderson College as a young music teacher. In 1959 she returned to visit Anderson College. On her list of persons she must visit were two living members of that class.

Often Miss Denmark had spoken of one of her dreams—a dream unfulfilled. She had dreamed of establishing a home for retired women. The home would not be a charitable institution. Its purpose would be to give security and companionship to women of education and culture, alone and perhaps a little stunned and emotionally overwhelmed by retirement.

The house at South William Street in Goldsboro was not large enough to serve as the home Miss Denmark had envisaged. Enough that for the time being it sheltered, besides Miss Denmark, the retired Miss Cronkhite and two younger teachers who had terminated their careers at Anderson College.

With the long illness of her former teacher, Miss Denmark's duties were clear. Once more she followed a schedule, a schedule dictated by the needs of Miss Cronkhite, the patient. The tremendous appeal of Anderson College, which had motivated her life for years, faded into the background.

There was time for prayer, for the singing of hymns with the frail patient, time for soul searching. New spiritual meanings were discovered as Miss Denmark thought of the universality of sorrow, of death, of growth that continues beyond death. Realizing that out of pain and suffering one discovers new answers to age-old questions, she commented, "I am certainly learning lessons in the laboratory of life. I am finding that His grace is sufficient for every need."

Then Miss Cronkhite slipped away and left an emptiness in Miss Denmark's life. Anderson College no longer needed her services, and her days of tender care of Miss Cronkhite were over. Miss Denmark possesses a warm, affectionate nature which has always attracted devoted friends to her. Love plays an important part in her life. Tears came to her eyes often during those first days of aloneness whenever she talked about Miss Cronkhite. They were not tears of self-pity, but tears of love and tenderness for one who was missed.

Neither did Miss Denmark mourn as one without hope. Often she had reminded Anderson College students in chapel talks that sorrow would come sooner or later to their lives. She had written to a friend after the death of her only sister, "We cannot call a person lost if we know where she is."

Miss Denmark is the last surviving member of the older generation of her family. Visits in the homes and over the telephone with nieces and nephews consume many hours. One nephew was still in college. The activities of students would always attract her. For William Denmark she became a mentor and an inspiration during his days at Wake Forest.

But Miss Denmark was still a part of Anderson College. She always would be. Not that she'd ever try to dictate policies to the new administration. She had left Anderson so that they could never say that about her.

Now that she had leisure she began to write more often to her girls. She had a hobby that she enjoyed—writing postal cards and occasional short letters. She couldn't write much to so many girls. Over the years there had been hundreds of girls. One summer at Ridgecrest she bought a package of one hundred dogwood cards to mail and she buys and mails many Chautauqua prayer cards.

These girls had been dear to her, very close, some of them for four years. Anderson College was a senior college when she went there as piano teacher in 1917. It was still a senior college when she became dean of women, but it became a junior college when she became president in 1928 [1930]. In a junior college a girl stays only two years. She is soon gone and living a life of her own. But the close association in a small college was not soon forgotten.

Before retirement, cards at Christmas had to suffice. Even now letters were impossible most of the time, but much can be written on postal cards.

Mary Lou Salla Mitchell was an only child. When her mother died, she was alone in the world except for her husband and three sons. She writes a letter every Sunday to Miss Denmark, sharing news of her family and church work.[31]

Then there is Elizabeth Tribble who was closely associated with Miss Denmark, first as a student for four years and then as a staff member of the college. A member of a big family she is now at home alone except for a sister. Though holding an important executive position, she writes daily, sending news of Anderson College and Anderson.

Retirement has made it possible for Miss Denmark to send cards to these and to others. She writes letters of congratulation, sympathy, and encouragement. She remembers birthdays, anniversaries, and special occasions. [both Ebenezer and Gethsemane.]

This picture of Anderson College's campus shows the West Dormitory, which would eventually be known as Denmark Hall. Photo is located in the 1948 *Columns*, page 5.

To one of her former faculty members whose mother had died several years before she wrote, "I am thinking of you today, April 14. I remember that this was your mother's birthday. I never met her, but I felt that I knew her from what you told me about her."

Letters of condolence have to be written frequently. Comforting letters are needed when sickness or disaster come to her former students. They remember her chapel talks and want her to know about what happens to them.

In a chapel talk to the students of Anderson College in 1941, Miss Denmark said, "I make it a point in my life to be happy in whatever I undertake, and this morning, April 8, 1941, I would rather be in the Anderson College chapel talking to you than anywhere else in the world."

In retirement in Goldsboro, the former president of Anderson College has said that each day is precious to her. She says that since returning she has missed the intellectual and spiritual stimulation of daily association with educational and religious leaders. "But that has been a blessing in its way," she declares. "Retirement has forced me to develop an eloquence of silence [to take memory vacations]. I have had to draw on inner resources, to stop talking to God and listen to him instead."

Dr. Solon B. Cousins, sending a Christmas message from his home in Richmond, Virginia, wrote: "When you retired at Anderson College you retired <u>from</u> something <u>to</u> something and that makes retirement an enriching experience."

"I am glad I came back to Goldsboro to live," she has said. "I am happy here and would not want to be anywhere else. Today, right now, is the only time that is ours." She ascribes to the belief that "the quality of one's life depends on the things he leaves behind and the things he carries with him."

It was in one of her chapel talks that she told the Anderson College students that she never saw a violet without thinking of Sidney Lanier's, "Lie down and put your cheek against the violet." She reminded the students, "It is no farther than that for your soul to climb to God. It makes no difference to flowers where they are planted or where they bloom. They bloom their very best, wherever they are."[32]

Chapter 14

Retirement Can Be Fun!

This is the day the Lord hath made; let us rejoice and be glad in it.
—Psalm 118:24

One Sunday in June, several years ago, Dr. Denmark stood at the door of her summer home in Ridgecrest and warmly welcomed friends from Anderson. She was spending her vacation in her beloved mountains.

In the group was a former student of Anderson College. For ten years Kathleen Cooke Withers had been almost blind. Following skillful surgery, she could see again. Affectionately she looked at her former college president and exclaimed, "You don't look a bit older than you did when I saw you ten years ago!"[33]

Miss Denmark smiled as she expressed her gratitude and happiness at the miracle of sight which had come to this courageous young matron. Miss Denmark is accustomed to comments on her failure to show aging. She likes to tell of an older friend who commented, "I wish I didn't look so well but felt better."

The grey has brought no great change in the silvery blond hair. Time has been kind to the fair complexion, an inheritance from her Viking ancestors. It sometimes comes as a shock to people much taller than Miss Denmark to learn that she is only five feet, six inches tall, for her dignified, statuesque bearing gives the impression of greater height.

With greetings disposed of that Sunday afternoon the conversation naturally turned to news of Anderson and Anderson College. Miss Denmark was interested in the campaign for funds in which the college at that time was engaged. One of the letters which had been sent to all former students had been written by her. Although her visits to the college have been infrequent since her retirement, she is still vitally interested with anything affecting its future.

But she has a variety of interests. Perhaps therein lies the secret of her amazing youthfulness. On that Sunday afternoon she led the conversation from talk about Anderson College to world events. Her daily schedule includes newscasts from favorite commentators. Walter Cronkite (the "h" has been dropped), great-nephew of her friend and colleague of many years, Miss Grace Louise Cronkhite, is included among these favorites.

A caller remembers hearing Miss Denmark say, "I have just finished listening to the news. I hope you heard it also. Just think of the wonder of radio!"

On another occasion she exclaimed, "I'm keenly interested in politics! I was at Ridgecrest during recent political conventions and did not have a TV. During the campaign I stayed at a neighbor's house until after 2:30 a.m., listening to election speeches."

To supplement the newscasts over radio and TV she avidly reads two North Carolina and two South Carolina daily newspapers. And she makes it a habit to read the Sunday edition of the New York Times, turning first to the editorial section. Occasionally she reads the Wall Street Journal. She finds almost all of the newspaper interesting, the news stories, features, editorials, syndicated columns, and the sports page.

Miss Denmark's Saturday afternoons are set aside for watching ball games. Her fondness for baseball dates back to her girlhood when she went to games with her mother. Goldsboro had a Little League baseball team with Wilson and Rocky Mount in the league. Her mother found baseball and games of all kinds exciting.

There was a gap of years after those early games and then Miss Denmark retired and became a baseball fan over TV. She has said that she would rather miss a meal than a Saturday game. Because of her earlier background she still likes baseball better than football and basketball. "But I am studying to learn more about football," she acknowledges.

When she was in Ridgecrest in the summer before the First Baptist Church of Atlanta acquired the [Ridgecrest] home which had been in her family since childhood, she watched the games with an octogenarian neighbor. But in 1962 she remarked, "Somehow I cannot get interested in baseball this year. Maybe I will later. The world situation seems so bad. I think it depresses me."

Eagerly she reads the sports pages of newspapers, but she never finds time to read the comic strips. She has a good sense of humor, however, and has at her command many amusing anecdotes. Her public addresses usually include several humorous and apropos stories. A favorite one is of the British [woman]

This picture of students playing basketball is located in the 1947 *Columns*, page 116.

member of Parliament who said that "she never knew what she thought until she heard what she said."

She also told of the woman who complained, "My husband has retired. I haven't. I am just tired." One of her favorite stories is of the little girl who said politely, when she received a pincushion for Christmas, "Thank you [Grandmother]. I always wanted a pincushion but not very much."

She is never at a loss for a timely comment. She likes to tell of the woman who was so clever that she always began her conversation with repartee. She has also admitted to audiences that her impromptu speeches are always well-thought-out in advance.

In 1940, Dr. Walter Crosby Eells invited Dr. Denmark to speak briefly in a session of the American Association of Junior Colleges in Columbia, Missouri. She told the group that Dr. Eells had invited her to speak on the subject, "The Problem of Student Scholarships," because she had reported that the basic problem of Anderson College concerned money, and it was necessary to give most of the students service scholarships.

Then she added, "As I have come nine hundred miles to this session and am to speak five minutes on the assigned topic, I feel like Mark Twain, one of my favorite authors, when he said, 'All anybody needs for success in life is confidence and ignorance.'"

A former student chatting with Dr. Denmark spoke of a chapel talk she had heard her make in which she had shared her collection of limericks. She asked if she still pursued the hobby of collecting these nonsense verses.

"Yes, if I can find amusing ones," she admitted.

In her collection are limericks gathered from reading and others donated by friends. She has recent ones of Ogden Nash and older ones dating back to Oliver Wendell Holmes and Edward Lear.

While listening to radio or TV programs, Miss Denmark frequently crochets or knits. "I like making afghans because it is creative work," she has said. "It is therapy for me. I enjoy designing ones with many colors, blending the colors that go together. I have made as many as four in one year for relatives and friends."

Miss Denmark tells a story about an afghan which she made a number of years ago for Mrs. Charles Sullivan, Sr., a benefactor of Anderson College and composer of the words and music of the Alma Mater. Mrs. Sullivan prized the afghan so highly that she willed it to her granddaughter and namesake, Luta Bewley Sullivan.

Luta Bewley was a child when her grandmother died and her mother, Coy Meeks Sullivan, tried to break the news gently. Luta Bewley listened politely, but impatiently. When her mother had finished she asked eagerly, "Mother, can I bring my afghan home now?"

Miss Denmark makes fewer speeches now. But she still takes notes when she hears sermons or lectures that she enjoys. And she marks for future reference her devotional books as she reads them.

She shared with a friend a devotional book she had read in the spring and summer of 1960. Apologizing for the marginal annotations, she commented, "The markings of my books makes them autobiographical. Sometimes they are too autobiographical for lending, for I sometimes have names of friends written in the margin."

Indicating her interest in learning more about the Holy Spirit, in the margin of one devotional she has written, "The power of the Holy Spirit! I have had experiences today with Him."

"Excellent on prayer! Poetic! Beautiful!" are other epithets describing her responses to what she has read. "Study and learn" is written often in the margins. A niece has requested that a certain one of her devotional books be willed to her.[given away many]

During a recent Christmas season she remarked to a friend, "Constant groping, searching, seeking. This is my life. Ye must be born again each day."

Attending a School of Christian Studies at Meredith College, she wrote to a friend, "We are indeed stretching our hearts and minds. We had a great time at Meredith—deep tortuous thinking but excellent."

In a speech [to the alumnae 1934] at a commencement service at her Alma Mater, Meredith College, Dr. Denmark spoke as usual about growth:

"We go to school a long time—some eighteen or twenty years all told," she reminded the students. "Then comes the end of so-called school. On the other hand we are just ready to begin our education, for there is a difference between schooling and education. It is possible to have a good deal of either without getting very much of the other. Schooling ends; education does not end...I believe in growth, in continuous everlasting growth."

In her notes to friends she often sprinkles such bits of wisdom, "God is surely unfolding His life in each one of us—We must be still in His presence and let Him do what he wants to do with each of us."

It is not surprising that the woman, who knew Miss Fannie Heck as her Sunday school teacher and who served from 1938 to 1953 as a trustee of what was then the W.M.U. Training School, prayerfully accepted the challenge when she was asked in 1960 at the age of seventy-two to serve as president of the W.M.S. of the First Baptist Church of Goldsboro.[34] She continued in this office for two years, but she has had to turn down many invitations to serve. She has commented that one of the compensations of being past seventy is that one can say, "No."

Recently she wrote to a former colleague, "I am interested in your many activities. My ministry today is largely limited to letters and the telephone." She could have added, "and to prayers." In another recent letter she wrote, "There is no slowing up in my interest and love for my friends."

Years before Miss Denmark retired as president of Anderson College, she had impressed her two Goldsboro nieces, Mrs. Charles Crawford and Mrs. John Henderson, with the importance of prayer. These young matrons passed on their interest to others. A prayer group, one of the Frank Laubach cells, was organized in Goldsboro, meeting weekly in the homes of participating members and playing a significant part in the lives of Goldsboro women. With her retirement Dr. Denmark became a member of a group which met one morning a week for prayer in place of bridge. One year, Christmas through August, she spoke on the Holy Spirit in a series of talks.

When asked about the special problems of the aging, Dr. Denmark said that one problem of some older people was that of having too much time.

"But I don't have enough time to do all the things I would like to do," she said. Another problem that an older person may face is that of being dependent on other people, according to the former college president.

"I have friends and relatives who are good to me, but I now have to depend on others for many things. Of course loneliness is another hurdle to be faced by the aged. My sister-in-law has been worried because her teen-aged grandchildren no longer like to come to spend the night in her home."

After reading a book on aging, Dr. Denmark said she wished she could give talks on the subject to older people. She describes retirement as a rich and satisfying time. She has worried that some of her friends may have unwisely postponed their retirement, fearful of the emptiness that may lie ahead of them.

Although not recommending it for everyone, she could tell her older friends of one most satisfying activity, that of reading the New Testament in French. Miss Lucas, her long time friend and housemate, is a student and former teacher of languages. When Miss Lucas began to read the New Testament in French, Miss Denmark, eager to find new insight into the scripture, refreshed her knowledge of French and joined Miss Lucas in the fascinating study.

But bird watching is a pastime that young and old can enjoy. Miss Lucas has become a friend of every type of bird known in the Southeastern states. Dr. Denmark and Miss Lucas pursued the hobby of bird watching while at Anderson College. There they had a special pair of cardinals they fed regularly. One morning they noticed an unusual call of strain and alarm from the cardinals. Looking closely at the cardinals on a twig outside the window, they saw a young cardinal not yet able to take care of himself.

The two older birds would fly toward the window where their friends watched and then back to the twig by the little bird. Miss Lucas said it took her some time to understand that what the older birds were saying was that they had their own family to look after and that she and Dr. Denmark would have to come for the little fellow. They did and brought him through with milk and bread. For years afterward when they walked the wooded campus, that bird would accompany them, hopping along near them as tame and sociable as a family dog.

From Goldsboro comes another bird story. During Hurricane Hazel,[35] the storm lashed at Goldsboro and ripped up many trees. Miss Katharine Culyer, a former Anderson College voice instructor, was watching the storm from the back windows of Miss Denmark's home, which faced the [St. Paul's] Methodist church. Miss Culyer called that the church steeple was swaying, about to fall. By the time Dr. Denmark arrived the steeple had fallen. At the same time, at the bird feeding station outside the windows, a chickadee came and helped himself to some seeds, oblivious to the storm.

Miss Denmark wrote in a letter to a friend of their watching in the back yard the "gorgeous birds, a flock of evening grosbeaks—eating sunflower seeds on the window-sill feeder. Also," she wrote, "from time to time can be

Miss Katharine Culyer taught at the college from 1928 to 1950 and from 1952 to 1953. For more information, see Appendix D.

seen Baltimore orioles, goldfinches, cardinals, mocking birds, robins, titmice, chickadees, and the brown thrush."

Dr. Denmark, retired administrator, has her own formula for being happy after retirement. It is a simple one; the mediums are available for any retired person. "Don't stop learning and growing. Keep the lines of communication open—with other people through cards and notes, the telephone, and service; with Nature through God's creatures; with the expanding world through radio, TV, and newspapers; and with God through prayer."

Chapter 15

"Prepare Me for What Thou Art Preparing for Me"

Be still, and know that I am God.
—Psalm 46:10

"A very old saying reminds us, 'All things come alike to all,'" Miss Denmark said in one of her talks. She continued, "Birth, life, death, joy, sorrow, all things do come alike to all, but all things do not come out alike to all. How they will come out, what they will do to us, will depend upon what things they find within us."

No college year passed at Anderson without death coming into the lives of some of the college family, students, faculty, or trustees. In her devotional talks Dr. Denmark tried to help the students to develop inner resources in preparation for the sorrows that must come to them. In the years since her active days in Anderson, she has had many occasions to write words of comfort to former students.

When Mrs. Charles S. Sullivan, Sr., widow of one of the founders of the college, died in 1944, Miss Denmark spoke at a memorial service for her.

"Mrs. Sullivan has entered a new day, but her consecrated life will linger with us to bless us and to help us journey on our way," she said. "She has given lavishly to Anderson College through the years, of her time, her strength, and her means. She has loved the college and borne it up in her prayers through all the years of its history. I shall always call her our Patron Saint."

Though often the necessity came to weep for others' griefs, Dr. Denmark always found victory and consolation in her Christian faith. She called Mrs. Sullivan a saint of the present day and said, "Death is not a subject we should seek to evade. People talk of death as an ultimate ending, when in reality it is only a door."

In paying tribute to Dr. Enoch W. Sikes, president of Clemson College and a trustee of Anderson College, she said:

"And I think that as Dr. Sikes passed into the great adventure on last Wednesday that he walked straight up to the gates of heaven, and with a salute, said, 'Lord, I'm ready for the next task.' For Dr. Sikes lived in an 'I am ready attitude.'"

In spite of grief over the great loss suffered in Dr. Sikes' passing, she said that "We can smile, and be joyous today for we know that our Dr. Sikes was ready to go to God. God is a spirit. The biggest part of us is spirit. Dr. Sikes' body is now gone, but his spirit is strong and ready to go back to its Maker. Dr. Sikes has just outdistanced us in the race of life."

She continued by quoting the words of Jesus: "Let not your heart be troubled; Ye believe in God, believe also in me. In my Father's house are many mansions."

"My friends," she said, "Jesus has told us that much about death. If we can believe that much about death, it is all we need to know. We can never know the truth and comfort of those words, until we have lost a loved one. Then we can put Jesus's words to the test and find how marvelously they work."

One year on the anniversary of her father's death, on July 18, she said, "We are told that each departed friend is a magnet that attracts us to the next world."

During the long illness of her friend, Miss Grace Louise Cronkhite, she wrote to a friend, "Miss Grace remains about the same—sleeps and sleeps—like the quiet prelude to the good Father's eternal journey's end." In another letter she wrote, "Miss Grace is no better. I am convinced that there is nothing this life brings that does not have spiritual significance and I am seeking and finding spiritual growth in all of this."

Of one of those close to her who had suffered tragedy, she said, "Death ushered her into the fraternity of those who sorrow." And in speaking of the mystery of suffering, she commented, "I am sure we all learn through suffering what can be learned in no other way."

She wrote about a hospital experience, "The only certain thing about trouble is that it will pass. There is a compensation for every trouble. We do not understand. We are not expected to understand, but we can lend ourselves in faith to such experiences."

In speaking of illness, she said, "How we need to realize that we are surrounded by invisible and spiritual power which is greater and more powerful than anything materialistic."

At a time of national tragedy she remarked, "It is all mighty sad to me, but God is at the helm and will counsel and guide all of us."

In one of her letters she called death "God's method in colonization, a transition from this world to the fairer and newer home."

Anderson College students will remember Dr. Denmark's reminder of the words of Dr. White, "O God, prepare me for what Thou are preparing for me." She quoted this in a recent letter and added, "God is very near me these days and I do feel that I can do all things in His strength."

It is not surprising that a woman who used "Growth" as the theme for so many of her talks, thinks of death as a step into an eternity of continued growth. She has said, "The truest end of life is to know the life that never ends."

When in her nineties Mrs. A.L. Smethers, the saintly wife of Anderson College's lifetime trustee, said that she believed that the only reason the Lord left her on earth so long was that he had not yet seen her become what he wanted her to become. [Exact? No]

Dr. Denmark echoed her words when she said, "The only justification for our continued existence here is the privilege of growing."

Note: The following chapter does not appear in the original manuscript that was edited by Miss Denmark. It includes additional information about Miss Denmark's last years and was revised and rewritten by Miss Copeland after Miss Denmark's death in 1974. It bears the original chapter title.

Chapter 16

...And Then She Taught

"Katharine Culyer died Tuesday and will be buried in a Boston cemetery. Claire and I had a prayer of rejoicing over her blessed release. She had been ill for two years—now her coronation. We cannot grieve for her. Death is just a fact of life."

The time was August 1973. In handwriting clear and distinctive, Miss Denmark wrote of the death of her friend and former voice teacher at Anderson College. She sat at a large desk in a sun-showered room with a large bay window, a room doubling as bedroom and office. She called it her laboratory. Elizabeth Allen, who dropped in daily, waited to take a few cards to the post office.

Mrs. Allen, speaking of her friend of many years, in a letter written to a friend of Miss Denmark's, said, "She looks much the same as always. There is little change in her once ash-blond hair, now gray. At eighty-six her fair skin is only slightly lined. But Miss Denmark, accustomed to administering the affairs of a college for many years has come to the place where she has to depend more and more on others. Arthritis has made getting about increasingly difficult."

Speaking of growing old, Miss Denmark said, "Although I do not call the last of life a prime time, I am learning to accept its experiences as necessary to complete the whole of life. We must recognize death, too, as part of our destiny. Why is it so difficult to accept the inevitability of death? My faith also affirms the inevitability of eternal life."

Long before it became popular to bring death or dying into the open with a plethora of magazine articles, books, lectures, and seminars, Miss Denmark was telling college students that death was not a subject to be evaded.

This photo of Dr. Denmark is from the 1949 *Columns*, page 10.

She reminded them of the three young rioters in Chaucer's "Pardoner's Tale" who tried to hunt down their enemy, Death, to kill him. "You have no need to imitate them by rebelling against your mortality with acts of violence. Facing the reality of death can serve to make life more precious for you."

Hoping to assist undergraduates in building inner resources, she went back to a very old philosophy, "All things come alike to all. How things will come out, what they will do to us, will depend upon what things we find within us."

She chose an honest approach to death. "I know I am going to die. We are born to die but we are born to have abundant life." And of one who had died she said, "She will go into the new life which we all will do one day."

It is easy to think of life on a college campus as connoting springtime, commencement, aspiration. Death is a thing alien, incongruous, inconceivable—that only happens to others.

"Death did not spare our young people," Miss Denmark remembered. "Death came into the lives of our college family: undergraduates, teachers, patrons, servants, trustees. When it came, I tried to offer comfort. Like all the suffering Jobs who have lived and died I searched for the meaning behind grief and pain."

Students needed courage to meet sorrow. Miss Denmark saw death choose a carefree teen-ager ushered overnight from a paradise where nobody died into a harsh, new world; an adolescent watching a hideously painful disease slowly destroy her mother; sisters unable to understand why polio struck down a brilliant older brother on the eve of his graduation from Clemson. She suffered with the young woman who worked in her office whose dreams were shattered by a message that her classmate and fiancé was dead, killed by a soldier he was taught to hate but might have liked if they had met between the wars.

Miss Denmark told her young charges, "Your heavenly Father not only keeps an eye on the sparrow but is very near to each of us when sorrow comes. God speaks to us through His acts and His acts speak of hope."

In spite of the mystery surrounding suffering and sorrow, she continued to see hope blotting out despair: hope in God showing his rainbow after rain; in the chanting of an Easter canticle; in Duke University students in jeans, sitting on the floor of their beautiful Gothic chapel singing "Amazing Grace"; in green ivy climbing on weathered walls; in a cardinal practicing arpeggios on a bare tree limb; in a student in granny glasses bent over books in a library carrel; in a woman with failing eyesight poring over the lines of Browning's "Epilogue to Asolando":

> *No, at noonday in the bustle of man's worktime,*
> *Greet the unseen with a cheer!*

She was sure all was not right with the world, but she had faith in a God who is alive and active. "It is all mighty sad to me, but God is at the helm and will counsel and guide all of us," Miss Denmark wrote at a time of national tragedy. And in another letter she expressed her trust, "God is surely unfolding His life in each of us. We must be still in His presence and let Him do what He wants to do."

A note from a hospital bed to a friend read, "How we need to realize that we are surrounded by invisible and spiritual power greater and more powerful than anything materialistic. Think of the spiritual you. God is spirit. The spirit of God is within you."

Recommending the words of old hymns as better than tranquilizers for chasing away insomnia, she said, "In your weary night watches, try quoting the lines, 'The great physician is now near, the sympathizing Jesus.' Repeating Whittier's 'Immortal love, forever full, forever flowing free' can quickly lull you into a quiet sleep."

She said of hymns, "I love them—realize they were written out of somebody's experience—they mean much to me, always have. As a child we all gathered around the piano to sing hymns together on Sunday afternoons."

After Miss Denmark retired, Wilton E. Hall, Anderson publisher, invited her to contribute a weekly column to the Anderson papers, choosing selections from her speeches or composing commentaries on current happenings. "I hesitated only briefly," she said, "before declining the opportunity to reach readers in Georgia and South Carolina through the widely circulated newspapers. I felt that this was not the best way to spend my time.

"I worked daily with notebooks, cards, and letters. My correspondence seemed to increase with the years, and after I retired I had no secretary. When the letters requesting recommendations dropped off, I resolved to reduce my correspondence. But letters from former students kept pouring in, and I could no more disown those members of my family by failing to answer their messages than I could hang up the telephone on one of my many nieces, nephews, or great-nieces and -nephews. Thus the writing of letters and cards became a large part of my witness and testimony.

"I used to work in my room for at least three hours a day, but in my eighties I had to slow down, to take a vacation from much of my writing. But the writing of letters to my family of former students and faculty and friends and the making of notebook anthologies are the things I loved to do. In sharing thoughts distilled from a lifetime of observation, mediation, reading, and study, I put to use any creative energy I possessed."

Those receiving one of her gifts could turn the pages of an artistically arranged notebook, tessellated with quotations from a variety of sources: philosophy from Marcus Aurelius, Socrates, and Seneca; meditations of Saint Augustine, Saint Teresa, and Saint Francis. Representing world literature, were quotations from Tolstoy, Goethe, Hugo, and Ibsen. Shakespeare's lyrics and Browning's dramatic monologues provided gold and lapis lazuli for mosaics designed from English literature.

An Anderson physician evidently found therapeutic value in his gift. "I keep the book on my bedside table where I can read it each night before going to sleep."

Paradoxically Miss Denmark wrote on a note to a friend, "It is pathetic to grow old, but I like it."

As she worked hard to finish the last of her notebooks, she continued to call old age a satisfying time of life. But she did not gloss over the suffering that often accompanies age. Without rereading the book of Job she had lived long enough to perceive that suffering does not discriminate between the righteous and the unrighteous, and she also perceived that when Death comes with an unexpected summons or tarries before bringing release from a painful, lingering illness, Everywoman shares equality with Everyman.

In her eighty-fourth year she wrote the following birthday message to a friend: "I hope it will be a very happy birthday for you and that you may have as many more as you would like! I can tell you that each increasing year brings increasing struggles and frustrations of the physical, but isn't it glorious as we do go down physically that we can aspire to be pushing up spiritually? Claire and I are making a real game of trying to convert physical handicaps into a triumphant experience. So far we are succeeding—I hope."

She awarded Claire commendation as a winning player, "Claire seems more spiritual than physical."

The game the two of them played could be called a musical game. No longer could anyone hear Miss Denmark fingering the keys of her piano with her loving, artistic touch. The house on William Street had grown much quieter after the day when Miss Culyer stopped practicing her voice lessons to depart for the University of Indiana to continue her study of voice, assisted by a small legacy left her by Miss Cronkhite.

But Miss Denmark remained conscious of the rhythms of life. Now the tempo was slow and there were many rests. In the night watches she could draw upon an inner world of beauty sculpt from such stuff as the evocative phraseology of the Scriptures or the music of great poetry.

She sent a Browning birthday greeting to a friend late in 1973, writing: "I saved this for you. I have always loved the quotation."

The words of Browning's *Paracelsus* had appeal for age as well as youth. Perhaps she was thinking about proving her soul in the suffering and dying she recognized as part of the human condition. Perhaps she was thinking about a flight from the memories of the past and in the moment of the present into the mysterious future, controlled for bird and man by the God who created them.

I go to prove my soul!
I see my way as the birds their trackless way—
I shall arrive! what time, what circuit first,
I ask not: but unless God sends his hail...
In some time, his good time, I shall arrive;
He guides me and the bird. In his good time!

Appendix A

I Like "How Green Grew the Ivy!"

Tuesday Night
Dear Kathryn,

The manuscript came yesterday and your letter arrived this morning. I am hastening to send the copy of Ed's letter back to you. I think it is an excellent letter—well expressed, kind and considerate—I shall be interested in his response to it. You did not refer to my lengthy letter to you last week but I judge you received it. I mention it only because I tried to have you understand me in all of this. I know nothing of copyright rules etc. but I certainly think you should have large credit if you allow the college to use your material.

I have read the manuscript in its entirety. You certainly know how to write and do it awfully well. The fact that you have written so much about me, with so little communication or dialogue between us is remarkable. I do not believe we have ever sat down for an hour's interview and question about all these years. Some of the manuscript is poetic and beautiful to me. Much of it is journalistic in style (and I have none of that). There are a few additions and a few inaccuracies which we would have to discuss. Do you remember Mr. Frank McGee—and Mr. Sam Price—both of whom helped in resolving our financial crisis with Hibernia Trust Co.: I should like credit given to them along with Mr. Vandiver.

I wish, too, that somewhere you could include the remarks that Dr. Elliot made upon my influence living a thousand years. That meant much to me coming from him.

Wouldn't it be possible, also, to include the figure of $985,000, which we announced on Founders Day 1953 was ear-marked to A.C. from the Baptists of South Carolina? Then, I have so much of Dr. White. I wish more could be said about him. I have made slight markings on your manuscript where I have had thoughts of interest.

I presume all we can do now is to wait and see what the college does. I spoke of having Mary & Virginia to read your Denmark Story. They are so busy and so involved all the time. Mary was in Greensboro two days last week for the trustee-orientation program. She drove to Raleigh, left her car there and drove to Greensboro with Dr. and Mrs. Heilmare. This Saturday, Mary and Charles and Virginia are driving to Columbia—to be present when Alice's baby is baptized on Sunday a.m.

The last of this month Mary & Charles are going to Mexico—they will fly to Mexico City & radiate out from there. Their 40th wedding anniversary is April 12—and they will probably have a full year of celebration in a number of ways.

Miss Copeland was an Anderson College faculty member from 1926 to 1954. She also served as dean of faculty and was the author of "When Green Grew the Ivy." This photograph is found in the 1929 *Sororian*, page 11.

It is awfully cold to-night and freezing. We have called off Prayer group for to-morrow morning. Must close this now. Love to you always,

Dovie

P.S. I've just reread this letter to Ed. The possibility of Dr. Hester's history[36] would not make the printing of your manuscript remote!! Please let me have a copy of your final draft of the letter you send to Ed.

A.D.D.

Appendix B

The Denmark Story[37]
By Kathryn Copeland
CUE: ALMA MATER AS THEME MUSIC...FADE FOR ANNOUNCER

ANNOUNCER: Here's a drama written especially for the 25th anniversary of Dr. Annie D. Denmark as president of Anderson College. It is called the Denmark Story, and was written by Kathryn Copeland. It brings you episodes from the life of Dr. Denmark, president of Anderson College from 1928 to 1952. But here is Ruth Hill Howard, a 1928 graduate of the college, to tell you the story. (FADING) Let's listen:

RUTH: (quietly) I'm Ruth Hill Howard, Anderson College, class of 1928. I'm proud and happy to tell you the Denmark Story. But I'm sad as well as happy. Sad because the last pages of the Denmark-Anderson College story are about to be completed. On May 22 Dr. Denmark will present diplomas to the 1953 graduating class of Anderson College and then will retire after 25 years as president. On February 14 friends of Christian education from the community, the state, and the nation will gather on the occasion of the birthday of the college to pay tribute to Dr. Denmark. But here is the Denmark Story as I know it.

I've been sitting here in the colonnade of the college in front of the fireplace looking at my memory book and my diary. Seems as if I've never been away. It is difficult to realize that on February 14 we'll be celebrating Dr. Denmark's 25th anniversary as president of Anderson College.

I came to Anderson College as a student in 1924. Dr. John E. White was the president and Miss Annie Dove Denmark was the dean of women. She often told us girls about how she first came to Anderson College as a piano teacher...(FADING)...That was away back in 1917.

MUSIC: Piano up strong in finish of Beethoven's "The Moonlight Sonata"

CHRISTINE: How did I play "The Moonlight Sonata," Miss Denmark?

DENMARK: That was the best you have ever played it, Christine. I consider you well prepared to play in the recital Friday night. I know you will make me proud of you.

CHRISTINE: It isn't true is it, what they're saying about you?

DENMARK: What is that, Christine?

CHRISTINE: They say you are not going to teach next year.

DENMARK: Dr. White has asked me to give up my piano teaching to be the dean of women at Anderson College.

CHRISTINE: What will become of me and your other pupils?

DENMARK: Christine, you have made excellent progress with your music. I predict that someday Miss Christine Scott will be known as an outstanding music teacher right here in Anderson. I shall recommend to Miss Grace Cronkhite, head of our music department, that she take you as one of her music pupils next year. That is one of the nicest things to happen to any piano pupil. Miss Cronkhite is one of the best teachers a girl can have. I know because she was my teacher when I was a student in Meredith College. Music was my first love, but if Dr. White thinks...(FADING)...I can best serve Anderson College as dean of women...

MUSIC: Anderson College "Alma Mater." FADING OUT

RUTH: I remember how Miss Denmark as dean helped us to develop a strong student government organization. She taught us to make student government true self government. When she talked to our student government association she never preached to us. She was frank to admit that since she and her generation had failed in many ways she did not presume to set herself up as a model. As I read my diary I can hear again her words to the student government association.

DENMARK: An old Spanish proverb says: "Take what you want; take it and pay for it." We can choose to be trustworthy or untrustworthy. When we choose good we have to pay for it in advance. Evil may be sold you on the installment plan. Often those whom we do not want to hurt have to pay our bills. I put the percentage of students who are living trustworthy, purposeful lives at 90% of the students in Anderson College.

CUE: MUSIC UP FOR INTERLUDE

RUTH: When I attended Anderson College my alma mater was a senior college for girls. While I was a student Dr. John E. White resigned as president of the college and as pastor of the First Baptist Church in Anderson. He went to a church in Savannah, Georgia. That transition period until a new president was chosen was a difficult time. Then one day the Board of Trustees of the College held an all-important meeting.

DR. SMETHERS: We have met today, gentlemen, to try to find a successor to Dr. John E. White who resigned after serving as president of Anderson College for ten years.

BOARD MEMBER: Dr. Smethers, it is going to be exceedingly difficult to find a man to succeed Dr. White. He is one of the most outstanding preachers in the Southern Baptist Convention. He has given so much prestige to the College as its president that it will be no easy matter to secure a man to follow him.

DR. S: We have considered several good men who have been recommended to us. We are still looking for the right man. We must choose a man who will emphasize the message which Dr. White always stood for..."the influence of the living soul as the supreme motive power, as against any and all intellectual attitudes."

SECOND B.M.: Dr. Smethers, does the president of Anderson College have to be a man?

DR. S.: I have in mind a person whose whole life is marked by a definite resolution to keep moral and spiritual values in preeminence. This individual loves Anderson College and has the same vision of Christian education which Dr. White has always had. I am referring not to a man but to a woman—Miss Annie Dove Denmark, dean of women of Anderson College.

SECOND B.M.: If any one can carry on the tradition of Anderson College as Dr. White did, Miss Denmark can. But will the people of South Carolina accept a woman as president of one of their colleges in this year of our Lord, 1928? After all women college presidents are few and far between and practically unheard of in the South.

DR. S.: Dean Denmark's faith in Christian education is strong enough to remove mountains as well as any prejudices which the people of South Carolina may have against a woman college president. Gentlemen, I think we have found a president for Anderson College.

<u>CUE: MUSIC UP FOR INTERLUDE</u>

RUTH: Thus the mantle fell upon the shoulders of Miss Annie Dove Denmark. Because she believed in youth, in their dreams, hopes, and visions, she dedicated her own youth to the task of leadership in Anderson College. We students were thrilled when our Dean was made president. We call her Dr. Denmark today, but she was Aunt Dovie to many of us during our undergraduate days. We thought of her as one of the most gracious and understanding personalities we had ever known. We were proud and happy when she presented the class of 1928 with their senior college diplomas at the commencement exercises. On that May Day in 1928 we were assured and self confident. There was nothing that we could not do. We'd make our names in the world. We remembered Dean Denmark's words from her first chapel talk with each incoming class of students.

DENMARK: When you graduate after four years spent at Anderson College your name ought to have some content and meaning. The alumni directory is full of scores of names of girls who have lived gloriously. You can write across your forehead a name which can be an honor to yourself, your parents, and your college.

MUSIC: "All Glory, Laud, and Honor"

RUTH: On February 14, 1929, Miss Denmark was formally inaugurated as the fifth president of Anderson College at the college's first Founders Day observance. Setting aside the birthday of the college, Valentine's Day, as a day to honor the founders of the institution was one of the traditions which Dr. Denmark began at Anderson College. Many of us came back for Miss Denmark's inauguration and for other birthday celebrations. Miss Denmark found the history of Anderson College a thrilling story and she loved to tell it to each succeeding group of students. The students may have thought that some of these dead people were more interesting than some of the people now living. Miss Denmark made the founders of Johnson Female Seminary sound so very interesting.

MUSIC: Hymn: "Faith of Our Fathers." FADE FOR:

CHAIRMAN: We are met today, brethren, to consider the establishment of a school for girls in Anderson village. As you know the tuition academies carry on most of our secondary education. The free public high school is known only in the most progressive communities.

CITIZEN: Mt. Holyoke was established in 1836. In Georgia there is also a school for girls, Wesleyan, established in that same year. If Macon, Georgia, can have a school for girls, why can't Anderson village? Here it is the fall of 1847 and we have made no provision for the education of our daughters.

SECOND CITIZEN: We must establish a college, but I think our college should be a Christian college.

CHAIRMAN: By all means.

THIRD CITIZEN: Since Baptists are more numerous than other denominations in the Piedmont section of the state, we can persuade the Baptists to support the institution.

CHAIRMAN: I know just the man for the presidency, Dr. William Bullein Johnson. He served as president of the Triennial Convention and he has advanced ideas on the subject of higher education for women.

DENMARK: Johnson Female Seminary opened its doors in February of 1848 with Dr. William Bullein Johnson, the first president of the Southern Baptist Convention, as the first president. It opened with four teachers and an enrollment of seventy students. Most of the students came from the Anderson District, but a number gave more distant addresses. A catalogue of 1848 gives us much interesting information about these students.

MARTHA VANDIVER: I'm Martha Vandiver from Anderson. Is your home near here?

AUGUSTA THOMPSON: I'm Augusta Thompson. My home is in Mississippi and it was no easy journey getting to Anderson. But I already feel at home here. I have met Mrs. Mary E. Daniel, the principal. She is a most attractive lady with a very charming manner.

SARAH RICE: I'm Sarah Rice from the Anderson District. I've very much taken with our eminent president, Dr. Johnson. He has taken a great interest in me and advised me that my course of study will include orthography,[38] reading, writing, elementary arithmetic, modern geography, construction of maps, moral philosophy, French and embroidery.

MARY WEBB: And I'm Mary Webb from the Anderson District. Of course before I came here Mother decided that I must take guitar lessons under Mr. William Wagstaff, a most romantic man. Just think, he was in the battle of Watterloo!

JERUSHA PRINCE: I'm from faraway Mississippi. I'm Jerusha Prince. I've been so lucky. I was able to secure a room here in Anderson with a lovely family. I like it better than staying in hotels as some of the girls are doing. For only $6 a month, I am furnished with good board, including washing, fire and candles.

DENMARK: Johnson Female Seminary prospered and became a University. The death of Dr. Johnson in 1862 was a severe blow to the university. The next year the doors of the school were closed, never, as it turned out, to be reopened. But the building that had housed its classrooms remained standing for many years. At least two schools, both of them locally famous, were conducted within its walls. The first was the Carolina Collegiate Institute;[39] the second was the Patrick Military Institute.[40] These schools were not failures.

They were spires of faith. Anderson College and its forerunners had the same ideal for the same community. The present Anderson College was founded as a community enterprise. On November 23, 1910, a meeting of leaders in the community was called at the courthouse in Anderson.

GENERAL BONHAM: Gentlemen, we have met this afternoon to carry forward our plans for establishing a college in Anderson. I will ask our secretary, Leon L. Rice, to bring us up-to-date on what steps have already been taken.

RICE: General Bonham and fellow citizens, you recall that the Chamber of Commerce met this spring to discuss the establishment of a college in Anderson. We all agreed that there was need of a college in combating the influences of materialism and industrialism upon the life of our town which is fast growing modern. At a second meeting on April 21 it was decided to canvass for subscriptions.

BONHAM: Thank you, Mr. Rice. I am happy to report that the canvass has resulted in the raising of $92,350. A.M. Carpenter also has an announcement for you.

CARPENTER: I am authorized by persons not present to announce that the goal of $100,000 has been reached.

BIZ: Applause and cheers.

BONHAM: The sole requirement which we have set has been that the college must be a Christian institution. Mr. Jolly,[41] as president of the Chamber of Commerce, what do you recommend as our next step?

JOLLY: The South Carolina Baptist Convention is meeting in Laurens. I recommend that W.R. Osborne, chairman of the committee appointed to canvass the situation concerning the establishment of a college, appoint a committee to go before the South Carolina Baptist Convention and offer the convention the $100,000 and the lot of thirty-two acres.

DENMARK: The South Carolina Baptist Convention voted unanimously to accept the offer of the citizens of Anderson and elected trustees. The charter was granted on Valentine's Day, February 14, 1911, and Anderson College opened for its first session in the fall of 1912.

ANNOUNCER: We have brought you the first half of "The Denmark Story," a special two-part drama written for the observance of the 25th anniversary of Dr. Annie Dove Denmark as president of Anderson College. You are cordially invited to be present on Saturday morning, February 14, at 10:30 in the Anderson College auditorium to join in the celebration of the 25th anniversary of Dr. Denmark as president of Anderson College. The second half of "The Denmark Story" will be heard tonight after station identification.

The Denmark Story—Part Two

ANNOUNCER: Tonight we bring you the concluding installment of the Denmark Story, a special two-part drama written for the 25th anniversary of Dr. Annie Dove Denmark as president of Anderson College. Here is Ruth Hill Howard, a 1928 graduate of the college, to tell us the story.

RUTH: Miss Annie Dove Denmark became president of Anderson College in 1928 and dedicated her life to preserving the traditions of Christian education begun in Anderson in 1848. She also had the vision and the courage to pioneer a new field of education in South Carolina. After a study of the practical educational needs of the community, the decision was made in 1929 to reorganize Anderson College as South Carolina's first junior college. That fall Miss Denmark came before the State Baptist Convention and asked them to ratify the transition to a junior college. She met unexpected opposition.

CUE: MUSIC UP FOR INTERLUDE

MODERATOR: The delegate here on my left has the floor.

DELEGATE: The Baptists of South Carolina do not need a junior college. These are difficult times and we need to preserve what we have. Why should we start a new type of educational institution? I do not think this convention should approve the changing of Anderson College to a junior college.

MODERATOR: Miss Denmark, would you like to tell the convention more about your reasons for wishing Anderson College to become a junior college?

DENMARK: South Carolina is crowded with four-year senior colleges. The Baptists of the state are trying to support four senior colleges for women and one university. Not every student can go to college for four years and not every student can profit by four years in college. I see in the junior college a democratic institution for the young people of South Carolina. It can be a good thing for the future of this state just as it has been a good thing for other states.

2nd DELEGATE: If we now have more Baptist educational institutions than we can support, we should not start a new type of institution. If Anderson College cannot secure adequate support as a senior college; then it should not ask us to continue to support it as a new type of institution.

MODERATOR: Opposition to a change of this type usually comes from the alumnae who do not like to see their college demoted from a senior college to a junior college. I wonder how the alumnae of Anderson College will accept this change. Can you tell us about this, Miss Denmark?

DENMARK: We do not consider that Anderson College has been demoted in becoming a junior college. Mrs. Olin D. Johnston of Spartanburg is in our audience tonight. She is a loyal alumna of the class of 1923. She may be willing to express her feelings about Anderson College becoming a junior college.

MRS. JOHNSTON: As I understand it Anderson College has already successfully made the transition from a senior college to a junior college. If Miss Denmark, the trustees, and faculty of Anderson College have had the vision to pioneer in the junior college field, we should commend them for their courage and wish them godspeed. I received my bachelor's degree from Anderson College, but I am proud that my Alma Mater is pioneering in the junior college movement. The change has been made so that the college can do a superior and distinctive type of work. Anderson College wishes to do more than simply duplicate the program of other colleges.

MODERATOR: It seems that the change has already been successfully completed. What do you wish to do about it?

BIZ VOICES: Cries of: Question!—Question!—Question! Sound of the gavel.

MODERATOR: All in favor of approving Anderson College as a Junior College, say "AYE."

BIZ VOICES: Aye! Aye! Aye! Gavel.

MODERATOR: Opposed say "no!" The ayes have it!

CUE: MUSIC UP FOR INTERLUDE

RUTH: Anderson College opened in September 1930 as a junior college. And that fall there were six boys as day students. The college took on new life and continued to thrive until 1932. Then the depression came. When Miss Denmark became the president of Anderson College the foundations of the business world had begun to totter and old institutions were wiped out over night. She inherited an indebtedness of $60,000, and annual payments of interest had to be paid. When the depression came, the mortgage creditors called for their money. It looked as if our college would have to close its doors. There was already speculation in some places as to how our beautiful 32 acre campus and our ivy covered brick buildings could be used when Anderson College ceased to exist. During those dark days President Denmark and Dr. A.L. Smethers, Chairman of the Board of Trustees, called the faculty into a special session.

DENMARK: When you became members of the Anderson College faculty I welcomed you to the joys and the burdens of Anderson College. I have asked Dr. Smethers to tell you briefly what we now face.

DR. SMETHERS: When Miss Denmark took over the presidency of Anderson College she also took over an indebtedness of $60,000. This indebtedness calls for the payment of $3600 annual interest. We are in the midst of a depression and denominational support has fallen off. We are helping as many students as possible to attend college but most of them need scholarships. Payments on the mortgage are due as well as the interest. President Denmark thinks there is one way in which we can keep the college open. Miss Denmark, will you tell the faculty about the one way which is now open to us?

DENMARK: A committee from the trustees went to New Orleans to talk with the mortgage creditors. They have agreed to let us continue to operate the college if we can pay the interest and begin to pay the installments on the mortgage. If enough of the faculty are willing to join me in working for whatever salary can be paid after the trust company is paid, we can keep the doors of Anderson College open.

MISS CRONKHITE: I joined the music department of Anderson College in 1917 at the same time that Miss Denmark came, and I want to stand by her just as long as she has faith that this college is filling a need.

DENMARK: I knew I could count on you, Miss Cronkhite.

MISS COWDRICK: I have been with the English department since 1920 and I would like to stay to see this thing through. I have always believed that it isn't what happens to you that matters but what the thing that happens to you does to you.

DENMARK: Miss Cowdrick, your many years of service to Anderson College are greatly appreciated.

WEBB VON HASSELN: I have been with Anderson College since the beginning, and I would like to continue teaching French and Spanish and German as long as I can serve the college.

DENMARK: Thank you, Mr. von Hasseln.

<u>VOICES: Cries of—"You can count on me."—"I want to stay."—"I believe in Anderson College</u>

DENMARK: You have indicated your desire to sacrifice for the cause of Christian education in Anderson College. You are majoring in things of permanent value—things which money cannot buy. You may receive five months salary instead of nine but you are rich. With such faith as yours Anderson College cannot fail. Our prospects are as bright as the promises of God.

<u>CUE: MUSIC UP FOR INTERLUDE</u>

RUTH: Bright days were ahead for my Alma Mater and for Dr. Denmark. As the president of Anderson College she frequently had to stand in the pulpit and speak for the college before the several thousand delegates who gathered each fall for the State Baptist Convention. Whenever it was possible I was present on the night when she was to speak. At first she was heard with some curiosity and even a little antagonism because she was a woman. It was not long before all of this changed.

MUSIC: "Onward Christian Soldiers"

MODERATOR: We now come to the part of our program concerned with our Baptist educational institutions. Miss Annie D. Denmark, president of Anderson College, will speak first.

DENMARK: Mr. Moderator and delegates to the South Carolina Baptist Convention. I am grateful for the privilege of coming before you to talk about our college at Anderson. The supreme purpose of our existence is and shall be the production of disciplined, devout Christian personalities. Anderson College will live as long as there are men and women who believe in Christian education.

VOICES: Cries of—"Amen!"—"That was a good talk"—"She's the best speaker we have in the convention."

CUE: MUSIC UP FOR INTERLUDE

RUTH: The story of Anderson College is a long story of "making bricks without straw," but today our College is free of debt. Miss Denmark saw the debt which she inherited paid off in 1938 by the South Carolina Convention and friends of the College. Shrewd business men of Anderson now have only praise for the level-headed business woman who proved their fears unfounded that a woman could not successfully manage the financial affairs of a college.

BANKER: I am an Anderson banker. I can truthfully say that Anderson College is one of Anderson's greatest assets. It adds to the purchasing power of the community and is being efficiently operated. Dr. Denmark, who took it over when it was practically broke, has done an excellent job in carrying on the work in a businesslike manner.

BUSINESS MAN: I operate several business houses in the Piedmont section. Anderson College is big business. Anderson College touches every angle of business life in Anderson. There are few commodities in Anderson for which Anderson College is not in the market at some time. The college places business on a higher level in Anderson. The efficiency with which the college handles business sets a standard.

CUE: MUSIC UP FOR INTERLUDE

RUTH: The denomination with which Anderson College is allied appreciates Miss Denmark's contribution to Christian education. She has served for several years as a trustee of the Woman's Missionary Union Training School in Louisville, Kentucky.

RUTH: In 1941 Furman University bestowed upon her the honorary degree of Doctor of Letters. Other groups also recognize her ability as a leader. In 1934–35 she served as President of the Southern Association of Colleges for Women, the first woman to hold such a position.

CUE: MUSIC UP FOR INTERLUDE

RUTH: As I read my diary and look back over my associations with Miss Denmark, I am immediately struck by the many hobbies and interests with which she has enriched her personality. She used to tell us about her hobby of taking notes and making scrapbooks.

DENMARK: One of my pet avocations had been the making and keeping of scrapbooks. I know I am not exaggerating if I say I have 100. It is one of the things I enjoy and can lose myself in.

RUTH: She is modest about her own achievements but always admired her predecessor, Dr. John E. White. She considered him a profound thinker and a great orator. From notes taken from his chapel talks and sermons she prepared the manuscript for a book, White Echoes, which was published by the Sunday School Board of the Southern Baptist Convention. The Anderson College students who came after me never knew Dr. John E. White in person, but they felt as if they had known him because Miss Denmark used quotations from Dr. White in many of her chapel and radio talks.

DENMARK: Dr. John E. White used to say, "God needs you just as much as you need him." He cannot make the world better except as he makes you better. He needs you.

MUSIC: PIANIST PLAYS. FADE FOR:

RUTH: Music is not just a hobby with Miss Denmark. She chose music as a vocation and studied piano for four years in college and for a year in New York. She taught piano at Buie's Creek Academy, Tennessee College for Women, Shorter College, and Anderson College. Then Dr. White asked her to become dean of Anderson College, and she turned a sharp corner in her life. She gave up music as a career. She never gave up her love for music.

MUSIC: PIANIST CONTINUES. FADE FOR:

DENMARK: "Music takes us to the edge of the infinite and lets us gaze thereon." What the musician is playing is going out on the ether waves all over the world. The musician is making a deposit, giving a part of himself.

RUTH: Although Miss Denmark has not had time to teach music since she took on a greater responsibility, the students of today understand something of her love for music. They understand when she begins on the first day of December to play Christmas carols for them in the dining hall at the dinner hour. They understand when Friday chapel is set aside for music. I understand what Anderson College stands for in music and that is why I sent my younger sister here for her junior college training.

CUE: MUSIC UP FOR INTERLUDE

DENMARK: When I first came to Anderson I taught a Sunday School class of older women, and those women were a great blessing to my life. I think one of the great needs of our time are homes for older people, real homes where these lonely persons can be comfortable and feel wanted. One of the great sorrows of my life is the fact that for many years we had no money to provide a retirement plan for our teachers. I am happy that I could remain at Anderson College to see us put into effect such a plan. Now that we have such a plan I would like to set an example by retiring after my 25 years of service as president.

RUTH: As Dr. Denmark has often told us: "Life is a mixed cup," and our joy on this anniversary occasion is mingled with sadness as time shuts another door behind us. But Dr. Denmark was never one to be afraid of what the years may bring. She always had the apt reply when we sang to her on her birthday:

<u>MUSIC:</u> "Happy birthday to you
Happy birthday to you
Happy birthday, Dr. Denmark,
Happy birthday to you."

DENMARK: "Oh me, Oh my, how times does fly,
And birthdays come as the years go by!
But never you mind; don't grieve about 'em,
'Cause you wouldn't be alive
If you went without 'em."

RUTH: The Denmark Story will not end in May 1953. It has become a part of the story of hundreds of Anderson College graduates who have gone out to become teachers, missionaries, secretaries, nurses, homemakers, and business and professional men and women. We realize that we have a philosophy of life adequate for our needs—a philosophy of life based upon such eternal truths as these oft-quoted ones of Dr. Denmark:

DENMARK: What do you want to become? You don't have to stay the way you are. You are not a finished product.

The quality of our lives depends upon the things we carry along with us and the things we leave behind. The New Year is a good time to sort out.

There are such divine possibilities within you. You are not a nobody. Everybody matters because nobody needs to stay as he is today.

The prospects for Anderson College are as bright as the promises of God and just as realizable as our obedience to those promises.

<u>MUSIC: Anderson College "Alma Mater"</u>

Appendix C

One of the first female physicians in upstate S.C., Dr. Olga Valeria Pruitt was born November 2, 1884, in Anderson, South Carolina, the daughter of Robert William Pruitt and his wife Minnie Riley Pruitt. Robert Pruitt was a local merchant. She began her education at Winthrop College and then went to the Women's Medical College of Baltimore and did her internship at the Medical College Hospital in Philadelphia, Pennsylvania. She completed post-graduate work at Johns Hopkins. The only woman in a field of 108 candidates for the state medical board examinations, she came to Anderson in 1911 and opened a private practice along with her brother, Harrison Pruitt, who was also a physician. In 1913 she also became the physician and professor of hygiene and physiology at Anderson College, serving in that capacity until 1956. Her heroic efforts during the 1918 flu epidemic greatly helped the community as well as kept the college open without the loss of a single student's life. She died in 1970 at the age of 85. Dr. Pruitt was inducted into the Anderson County Hall of Fame at the Anderson County Museum in 2004.[1]

[1] "Anderson College's History Reflected in 2004 Anderson County Hall of Fame Inductees," *Anderson College Today*, Fall 2004, 22; "Anderson University to Celebrate Founder's Day," *Anderson Independent Mail*, February 7, 2010, 5a; "Scholarship Fund Honors Longtime AC Physician," *Anderson College Today*, April 1998, 1, which also notes that Olga M. Orr, a relative and namesake, wrote a biography of Dr. Pruitt in 1978. See also Hester, *They That Wait*, 33.

Written by Dr. Joyce Wood, Anderson University history professor

Appendix D

Katharine G. Culyer was invited to join the faculty of Anderson College in 1928. Her friend, Grace Cronkhite was then Dean of the Music Department. Miss Culyer taught voice and Solfeggio and was director of the Anderson College Choir until she retired in 1953.

She was born February 17, 1898, and grew up in Purdys, New York. After her retirement in 1953, Miss Culyer moved with Dr. Denmark, Grace Cronkhite, and Claire Lucas to Goldsboro, North Carolina, where Dr. Denmark owned a duplex. In the fall of 1955, Miss Grace died, and Katharine, having no family, enrolled in a graduate studies program. She never received a formal high school diploma, but was so well-read and self-educated that she was admitted to the Indiana University School of Music for further study. She began in January 1956 and finished with both a Bachelor of Music degree and a Master of Music degree in 1958. She continued teaching and being involved with music until her death in 1973.

Miss Culyer was a fine musician and a dedicated teacher. Under her direction the Anderson College Choir became recognized as one of the best in the region and served as an effective ambassador for the college. Her students often sang at community functions. The full choir frequently visited other schools in the area and once joined in a mass choral concert with the South Carolina Symphony Orchestra in Columbia.

The Christmas programs—First Night and Vespers—were the highlights of the year. Realizing that they would usually hear new and special music, audiences always filled the auditorium. Miss Culyer introduced the now familiar "Carol of the Bells" and "Lo! How a Rose E're Blooming." In 1952 she and the choir presented excerpts from the challenging "Ceremony of Carols" by Benjamin Britten.

Katharine Culyer's presence at Anderson College, especially during the Depression and war years, greatly enhanced its vitality. Her work enriched the artistic life of the college and community and contributed immeasurably to the growth and prosperity to come. She should be remembered not only as a gifted teacher, but also as a very significant part of Anderson University's long and honorable history.

Written by Charlotte Hendley Badger, Anderson College class of 1950

Appendix E

Tribute to Grace Louise Cronkhite

Do you still not understand? Are your minds closed? You have eyes: can you not see? You have ears: can you not hear?
—Mark 8:18, the New English Bible

This admonishment in the form of a question is a quotation from Jesus. At the same time it is a part of the philosophy of any great teacher, for as "beauty is in the eye of the beholder," so it is a part of the teacher's function to help her students see and hear the beauty of the physical, academic, and spiritual world into which they were born. Because Aunt Grace saw beautiful things and heard beautiful sounds, she was a great teacher. Her capacities for seeing and hearing were infinite, and she found a childlike pleasure and wonder in everything from the simple taste of a fresh cup of coffee or a fresh, crisp radish, and the feel and smell and sight of falling leaves on a chilly, autumn day, to the magnificence of a massive symphony orchestra and the challenge of reading a difficult new book. Part of the legacy she left within her friends and students was the ability and appreciation to see and hear the way she did. "It is so pleasant," she wrote once, "not to be so ignorant." And the challenge of not being so ignorant grows into a pleasure for those who find new beauties and new areas of learning as a result of her living influence. Because she saw, we, too, see.

Another part of her legacy was the determination toward excellence. She said, "One has to remain sincere, and to do the very best you can—to be slipshod, I just never could be. It was no credit to me. I was just made that way. Music requires everything to be perfect—it wouldn't sound like anything unless it were done perfectly. I'm so glad I took up music. There's a great deal in the Bible about music—nothing about poetry, but a great deal about music."—THE VERY BEST YOU CAN. Nothing else satisfied her. From time to time this caused a grief-stricken student! It even caused some fear and trembling for those students who were timid. But not one ever left her studio, or her presence without courage. She had no patience with half effort, and that lesson is permanently engraved with inspiration on the mind of every student she ever had, not only in musical achievement but in every area of life. "All that expresses good in action is the state of the consciousness and not a set of circumstances." The state of consciousness to draw upon the BEST that is within, no matter what, continues to live because of her example and because she taught it so well with so much love.

"Unless you are contributing something worthwhile to life, there's no use in living." In 1917 the great pianist-teacher Rafael Joseffy offered her a position in New York as his assistant. She turned it down because she felt that the need was greatest in the then small, obscure college in Anderson, South Carolina. It is hard to judge just how much fame and fortune she gave up by remaining here. But because she contributed so much of herself to us, it is a legacy from her to give back to the world everything worthwhile that is in us. Her philosophy has taught us so—not so much because she herself did, but because we learned from her that there is, indeed no use in living unless we did.

There was about her a certain sense of security in being her friend, for a fine idea, or worthwhile dream, or an unselfish action received her instant support and encouragement and help. She not only gave it. She lived it. When a friend and fellow colleague at the college experienced failing eyesight, Aunt Grace found out about it by way of the grapevine. Meeting the lady in the colonnade the next day, she said simply, "May I have the great privilege of reading your Baltimore Sun to you?"—and there commenced many long hours during many years of reading aloud to a friend. During the Saturday afternoon radio broadcasts of the Metropolitan Opera, she always invited students and friends to share it with her. And always there was Russian tea and cookies at intermission. To this day Russian tea still has the rich taste of Tristan and Isolde to me. But the understanding of that opera and many other operas came directly from her, who loved others with her head as well as her heart, and whose leading was never confined to the classroom.

But the greatest legacy of all can be best expressed by this quotation from Elizabeth Barrett Browning.

> *Earth's crammed with Heaven,*
> *And every common bush afire with God.*
> *And only he who sees takes off his shoes;*
> *The rest sit around and pluck blackberries.*

She saw God everywhere from the age of a small child, and took off her shoes. Through her we have also learned to go barefooted, and very few who ever studied with her, or knew her at all, were left to ever be content merely plucking blackberries.

This is our legacy.

This tribute to Grace Cronkhite was written by Helen Hendley Donnell for the 1966 unveiling of Miss Cronkhite's portrait. It was read at the celebration by her mother, Mildred Lide Hendley.

For the centennial, the Anderson University Theatre Department presented *The Denmark Story*. This play, written by Scott Kirk and funded by the South Carolina Humanities Council, starred Dr. Deborah McEniry, chair of the Theatre Department. *Courtesy of the Theatre Department.*

Appendix F

For the centennial, the Anderson University Theatre Department presented *The Denmark Story*, a play based on Dr. Denmark's time at and presidency of Anderson College. *The Denmark Story* was written by Scott Kirk and funded by the South Carolina Humanities Council. Dr. Deborah McEniry, professor of theater and chair of the Theatre Department, played Dr. Denmark. The play was directed by Dr. David Larson, professor of theater and dean of the College of Visual and Performing Arts. Pictured here are Greg Allgood and Dr. McEniry.

Notes

Foreword

1. The Denmark Society was founded in February 1944 to meet the need for a merit system in Anderson College. The three prerequisites for membership are a high standard of Christian character, a constructive quality of service or of leadership and a maximum degree of individual scholarship. 1944 *Columns*, 43.

Acknowledgements

2. Charlotte Hendley Badger and Helen Hendley Donnell are two sisters with lifelong associations with Anderson University. Their association started, in fact, before either of them was born. During her own college career, their mother, Mildred Lide Hendley, had Miss Cronkhite and Miss Denmark as instructors and, after graduation, taught music at Anderson College from 1918 to 1921. Although not actually related, the Hendley sisters grew up with a close relationship with "Aunt Grace," "Aunt Dovie" and "Aunt Katharine." Both attended Anderson's Preparatory and Junior College Programs, with Charlotte graduating from the high school in 1948 and the college in 1950 and Helen graduating from the prep school in 1951 and the college in 1953. See Appendices D and E.

CHAPTER 1

3. Founders Day was held on Valentine's Day. The school charter was signed on February 14, 1911. Hubert Inman Hester, *They That Wait: A History of Anderson College* (Liberty, MO: Quality Press, 1969), 18.
4. When the community of Anderson proposed the plan for a women's college to the Baptist denomination, it was already responsible for Furman University, Greenville Woman's College, Limestone College and Coker College. Anderson College was its fifth higher education facility but only the fourth college it created designed to educate women. Hester, *They That Wait*, 14.

CHAPTER 4

5. Grace Louise Cronkhite (1869–1955) was a native of Warsaw, New York. She taught Dr. Denmark during her years as a teacher at Meredith College (1906–9). The two women became lifelong friends. Miss Cronkhite came to Anderson College in 1917 as the dean of music, and she remained at the college until she retired in 1953. From news clippings on her death contained in the Memorial book made by Annie Dove Denmark.
6. Buie's Creek Academy was a small school near the town of Dunn, North Carolina. It became Buie's Creek Junior College and eventually Campbell University. Hester, *They That Wait*, 59; www.campbell.edu.

CHAPTER 5

7. Regina Cook Cowdrick began teaching at Anderson College in 1920. By 1924, she taught literature and composition. Ms. Cowdrick attended Demin University, Toledo Normal Training School and George Peabody College for Teachers. *The Sororian*, 17.

CHAPTER 6

8. Dr. Carlyle Campbell was president of Coker College from 1925 to 1936 and president of Meredith College from 1939 to 1966. The library at Meredith College is named for him. www.coker.edu; www.meredith.edu.

9. Dr. E.F. Haight was the president of Anderson College from 1953 to 1957. He received a doctor of theology degree from the Baptist Bible Institute of the New Orleans Baptist Seminary. He spent a great deal of his professional career teaching. He came to South Carolina to teach religion at Furman University in 1944, and a special committee sought him out to take over the presidential position at Anderson College. Hester, *They That Wait*, 113–14.
10. Gladys Atkinson was the wife of South Carolina governor Olin D. Johnston. She graduated in 1923 but retained close ties with her alma mater. She became a member of the board of trustees in 1935. *The Yodeler*, May 12, 1943, 1.
11. E.P. Vandiver was an Anderson College trustee from 1927 to 1941. Hester, *They That Wait*, 167. He was an Anderson banker who supported Annie Dove Denmark in "her determination not to give up" on the school. He did not want the institution to close down during its economic troubles. Hester, *They That Wait*, 89.
12. The Baraca Sunday school class still meets at First Baptist Church in Anderson. It is a radio ministry that began in 1934, also called Broadcasting for Christ. It reaches out to homebound members with hymns and gospel songs. www.andersonfbc.org.
13. Webb von Hasseln taught modern languages and violin at Anderson College from 1915 to 1962. Hester, *They That Wait*, 177.
14. Olga V. Pruitt was the college physician from 1913 to 1956. Hester, *They That Wait*, 175. See Appendix C for more information.

CHAPTER 7

15. William Lyon Phelps lived from 1865 to 1943. He was an American scholar and literature critic, most well known for introducing Russian novelists to American readers. www.britannica.com.
16. Jane Addams lived from 1860 to 1935. She was a social reformer best known for establishing the Hull House in Chicago, a social settlement or welfare organization designed to improve neighborhoods in need. www.brittanica.com.
17. Frances Willard (1839–1898) was a reformer who founded the Woman's Christian Temperance Union in 1883. She also led the national Prohibition Party. www.britannica.com.

CHAPTER 8

18. Claire Eleanor Lucas worked on the Anderson College administrative staff from 1942 to 1953. Also, she worked at the school as a student counselor, psychology teacher and the director of the Student Government Association. *AC Today*, Winter 1975, 5.

CHAPTER 9

19. Dr. Harry Clark was a member of the Furman University Education Department from 1925 to 1930 before leaving to serve as president of Judson College in Alabama. Furman University Archive intern Caroline Vereen.
20. Mr. Charles Starke Sullivan Jr. served at Anderson College from 1925 to 1939 as an instructor and secretary-treasurer. Mrs. Charles S. Sullivan Jr. served at the school from 1942 to 1943 and from 1946 to 1959 in the English and Business Correspondence Departments. Hester, *They That Wait*, 176.
21. The Johnson Female Seminary was created in 1848 and was considered "one of the most promising Baptist schools of the time." It was led by William Bullein Johnson. Hester, *They That Wait*, 8.
22. Reverend William B. Johnson was the first president of the Southern Baptist Convention, and he was influential in establishing this organization in 1845. He served as the president of Johnson Female Seminary. Reverend Johnson died in 1862, and the seminary closed soon after. Hester, *They That Wait*, 8–10.
23. Dr. J.A. Chambliss was a retired Baptist minister who taught English at Anderson College and was the first college president, serving from 1912 to 1913. Hester, *They That Wait*, 24.
24. The Seventy-Five Million campaign was a financial campaign that attempted to raise $75 million over a period of five years. Due to bad financial conditions in the community, not all of the pledges were paid, and $75 million was never collected. However, the "amount collected was far greater than anything ever achieved by Southern Baptists." Hester, *They That Wait*, 45.
25. Charleston Southern University, originally called Baptist College, was founded in 1964 near Charleston, South Carolina. www.csuniv.edu.

Chapter 10

26. The words and music of the Alma Mater were written by Mrs. Charles S. Sullivan Sr. in 1916. Hester, *They That Wait.*

Chapter 12

27. Baylor University, located in Waco, Texas, was chartered in 1845. www.baylor.edu.
28. Mercer University is located in Georgia and was founded in 1833. Dr. Spright Dowell served as president from 1928 to 1953. tarver.mercer.edu.
29. Blue Mountain College was founded in 1873 in Blue Mountain, Mississippi. Dr. Lawrence T. Lowrey was the grandson of the school's founder, General Mark Perrin Lowrey. www.bmc.edu.

Chapter 13

30. Dr. Denmark shared her home in Goldsboro with fellow retirees Claire Lucas, Grace Cronkhite and Katherine Culyer, a voice professor. They all left Anderson College in 1953. *AC Today*, 5.
31. Mrs. Mary Lou S. Mitchell was a member of the 1930 graduating class. *Anderson University Alumni: Today* 2008, 547.
32. Stanley Lanier (1842–1881) was an American poet born in Macon, Georgia. www.britannica.com.

Chapter 14

33. Kathleen Cooke Withers was a member of the 1923 graduation class. *Anderson University Alumni: Today* 2008, 572.
34. The WMU (Woman's Missionary Union) was created in 1888. It is "the largest Protestant organization for women in the world," focusing on teaching and involving women of all ages in missions. www.sbc.net.
35. Hurricane Hazel hit the coast hard from October 14 to October 16, 1954. It caused property damage in North and South Carolina that totaled $60 million. www.i4weather.net.

APPENDIX A

36. Hubert Inman Hester wrote *They That Wait: A History of Anderson College*, which was published in 1969.

APPENDIX B

37. The original heading for this radio play reads: "3315—Problems in Radio Writing, Lessons 15 and 16."
38. Orthography is defined as "the part of language study concerned with letters and spelling." dictionary.com.
39. The Carolina Collegiate Institute began in 1866 under the leadership of Professor W.J. Ligon. It was for male students originally, but young women were allowed to attend starting in 1874. Hester, *They That Wait*, 8.
40. The Patrick Military Institute was moved from Greenville to Anderson in 1889 by Colonel John B. Patrick. It soon "became widely known and respected" in Anderson. When Colonel Patrick died, the school soon closed down. Hester, *They That Wait*, 8.
41. Mr. G.M. Tolly was the president of the chamber of commerce in the spring of 1910, when the community leaders began to plan strategies for raising the funds needed for the opening of a women's college. Hester, *They That Wait*, 12.

Index

P

S

V

W

About the Author

This picture of Kathryn Copeland is from the 1944 *Columns*, page 9.

Kathryn Copeland was born September 10, 1898, in Bolivar, Missouri, to Marion John Copeland and Pernettie Belle Barnes Copeland. An only child, Miss Copeland graduated from Southwest Baptist Junior College, obtained a diploma in religious education and a BMT degree from Southwestern Baptist Seminary in Fort Worth, Texas, and received her BA and MA from Baylor University.

Miss Copeland arrived in 1926 at Anderson College, where she taught Bible and English. While Miss Denmark was president of the college, Miss Copeland served as dean of the faculty during the transition to junior college status. She was later appointed dean of the college and served as recording secretary for the Board of Trustees. While on the faculty at AC, Miss Copeland helped to start the Beta Pi chapter of Phi Theta Kappa, a junior college honor society, in 1932 and served as its sponsor until her resignation.

As dean of the college, Miss Copeland officiated at "Denmark Day" at the Founders' Day Convocation on February 14, 1953, and served as secretary of the special search committee charged with finding a new president upon Miss Denmark's retirement. She left Anderson College in 1954 and moved to Gardner-Webb College in Boiling Springs, North Carolina, to continue her career before retiring to Charlotte, North Carolina. Miss Copeland died on August 16, 1977, in Huntersville, North Carolina.